MURDER AT ANNA BAY

MURDER AT ANNA BAY

The story of the investigation
into the murder of Judith Brown

JOHN SUTER LINTON

ABC
Books

First published by ABC Books for the
AUSTRALIAN BROADCASTING CORPORATION
GPO Box 9994 Sydney NSW 2001

First published in July 2008

National Library of Australia Cataloguing-in-Publication entry

Suter-Linton, John.
   Murder at Anna Bay : the story of the investigation into the murder of Judith
   Brown / John Suter Linton.

   9780733319068 (pbk.)

Brown, Judith.
Murder – New South Wales – Anna Bay – Case studies.
Murder – Investigation – New South Wales – Case studies.

364.1523099442

Cover by Luke Causby, Blue Cork Design
Internal design and layout by Judi Rowe, Agave Creative Group
Printed and bound in Australia by Griffin Press, Adelaide

CONTENTS

	FOREWORD	vi
1	9.14.28 A.M.	1
2	9.14 P.M.	27
3	KEEPING AN OPEN MIND	53
4	PERSONS OF INTEREST	67
5	NARROWING THE FIELD OF SUSPECTS	75
6	LIES, SUSPICIONS AND DOGGEDNESS	101
7	MISSING MONEY AND ODD BEHAVIOUR	127
8	MOUNTING EVIDENCE	143
9	BREAKING THE SILENCE	185
10	AGAINST THE ODDS	217
11	A CASE TO ANSWER	229
12	JUDGMENT DAY	235
13	MOMENT OF TRUTH	253
	POSTSCRIPT	261

FOREWORD

There are, on average, 200 murders committed in New South Wales each year. Most perpetrators are found with the 'smoking gun' in hand and brought to justice quickly. This means that police are able to establish a suspect's guilt through witnesses, irrefutable physical evidence, obvious motive, and/or confession.

But some murders leave police with nothing to indicate a clear suspect: no witness to the crime, nobody having overheard an admission of guilt or even been the assailant's confidant, no obvious motive, and several different possible interpretations of the physical evidence. These homicides run the risk of becoming 'cold cases'.

The homicide of Judith Brown in June 2000 is one such case.

When Detective Sergeant Peter Fox from Maitland Police attended the normally quiet seaside township of Anna Bay, he was faced with the bloody murder of a devoted mother of three sons, and a well-loved friend and neighbour. Despite an exhaustive examination of the crime scene, there were few clues. And while the start of the investigation was busy and well resourced with detectives, the reality of country policing is that after some weeks Peter Fox was left to solve Judith Brown's murder on his own.

Peter Fox's main support throughout the investigation came from the crime scene examiner Detective Senior Constable Peter Muscio. As the months went by, not a day passed when the two Peters failed to share theories, hoping to find the elusive piece of evidence that would identify a suspect.

This book describes in detail the investigation into Judith Brown's murder, revealing more than was ever presented to the jury. It is also the story of one policeman's dedication, professionalism and objectivity, his passion to see justice done for Judith Brown's family and friends, and his tenacity against the odds to bring the perpetrator to trial.

No witnesses, no motive and no confession ... just how did Peter Fox ever have enough evidence to secure a conviction against Judith Brown's killer?

Chapter 1

9.14.28 A.M.

Anna Bay is a quiet, picturesque coastal town situated on the mid north coast of New South Wales, roughly 45 kilometres north of Newcastle and just over 200 kilometres from Sydney. Freestanding homes and townhouses sit among a rugged bushland setting, which slopes gently down to the eastern shoreline. With its streets all walking distance to the local beach, Birubi Beach, Anna Bay makes an ideal location for retirees and those seeking a sea change. The village-like shopping area services locals with all the essentials, though for those wanting the diverse offerings that only large cities can provide, Newcastle is just an hour's drive away. During summer Anna Bay plays host to holiday makers who take advantage of the beaches, surf, and four-wheel-drive tracks.

Such is the parochial nature of the small town that most of the locals know each other, if only by sight, and newcomers don't remain strangers for long, particularly if they frequent the popular watering hole, the Anna Bay Tavern. It's this closeness and familiarity that gives the residents a sense of security. So safe do they feel that few bother to lock their front doors and some even leave their door and windows open during hot days to allow in the cooling sea breeze, luxuries afforded only to those living in such a community.

On a dark, overcast, and drizzly Friday 2 June 2000, this serene setting would be shattered. The residents of Anna Bay would quickly learn how vulnerable they were when one of their own, albeit a resident of just six months, would be found brutally murdered in her own home during the morning hours while everyone else went about their daily business.

As though forewarning the events to come, a low cloud cover brought intermittent rain and a chilling breeze to the area that day. Ross Brown, who had moved to 24 Clonmeen Circuit in January with his wife 39-year-old Judith and their three young boys, Gene aged 7, Joel 11 and Riley 15, arrived at his home at around 2.40 p.m. Forty-four-year-old Ross, who was semi-retired, had spent the day taking his dog, a Staffordshire terrier named Floyd, for a run along Birubi Beach, before settling in for the warmer surroundings of the Anna Bay Tavern to catch up with friends. He made sure, as he always had done, that he was home in time for his three boys' arrival from school.

When Ross returned home he was surprised to see his wife's car, a green Daewoo Numira hatchback parked in the driveway. Judith would normally have been at the Salamander Childcare Centre where she was employed as a childcare worker, not home until later in the afternoon. Ross alighted from his utility, a white Toyota HiLux dual-cab four-wheel-drive, and unclipped and lifted his dog down from the tray. He grabbed two

Toohey's New long-necked bottles of beer, which he'd purchased on his way home, and walked along the short path to the entrance. As soon as he unlocked the door the dog scurried inside. Ross Brown followed and was confronted with the sight of his wife, lying on the tiled floor of the foyer covered in blood. The beer bottles slipped from his grip and smashed on the floor, the frothy amber fluid spreading the blood further across the floor and towards the front door. Ross leaned down and slipped his arm under his wife's body, lifted her close and cradled her, talking to her, telling her to get up. He let out a scream. He had to get help.

Ross ran from his house to a neighbour's, where he rapped on and shook their front door violently for attention, all the time screaming that he needed help. Beth (not her real name) was confronted with Ross rubbing his bloodied hands over his face. She tried to ask him what had happened, to know whom to call. Ross, mumbling and growling to himself, was not being helpful. He even head butted and punched her wall and exclaimed, 'I've been down to the pub for a couple of beers and come home to this!'

He held out his bloodstained hands to Beth and yelled into her face, 'I've had a gutful of this … I can't handle this emotional sort of crap'.

Ross's behaviour unsettled Beth. All she could ascertain was that something had happened to Judith, but she wasn't aware of the severity of it. She guessed only that Judith was injured and required medical attention. Beth dialled triple-zero at 2.46 p.m., requesting an ambulance. The emergency operator could hear Ross shouting in the background as Beth nervously gave the address. Beth then followed Ross back to his house in case there was something she could do to help.

Beth knew Judith better than some of the other neighbours in the street. Judith would often call in to see her, share a cigarette, have a chat. They got to know each other and the area. It's possibly because of this relationship that Ross chose Beth to answer his calls of distress.

As Beth followed Ross back to his house, other neighbours began appearing, attracted by Ross's continued screaming. They stood cautiously at their front doors, trying to fathom what was going on. It was a busy time of day for Clonmeen Circuit: parents were waiting for their children to return from school. Another woman who lived in the street, Tina (not her real name), came forward and offered her help. Ross pointed to where Judith's body lay, shouting at the women, 'Help her … help her'.

Without warning Ross grabbed both Beth and Tina in a headlock, Tina under his left arm, Beth under his right, and tried to pull them inside the house to see his wife. Tina fought Ross's grip and broke free; Beth was too disoriented to fight. Tina waited outside. It wasn't long before Beth came running out, visibly traumatised by what she had seen. She vomited into the garden.

Ross re-emerged, yelling at the top of his voice, 'What a waste of twenty-odd years of marriage. What about my fucking boys?'

When the paramedics arrived Ross was pacing up and down outside his house, covered in blood and screaming abuse over what had happened to his wife. The ambulance officers followed departmental procedure and backed away to a safe distance. They weren't sure who Ross was or what he might have to do with the 'injured' woman inside. For all they knew, and certainly judging by his behaviour, he could have assaulted the woman and might be a threat to anyone trying to assist her. There was no point in taking a chance and risking their safety, so they put in a call to their dispatch requesting police attendance. There was nothing the paramedics could do until police arrived.

~

While the ambulance officers waited, the police dispatch centre contacted Nelson Bay police for uniformed officers to attend the scene at Clonmeen Circuit, Anna Bay. Nelson Bay was the closest police station to Anna Bay. Although details of whether the woman was the victim of an assault, was injured due to an accident or dead were unclear, detectives would also be required and they would come from Maitland Police Station. Anna Bay falls into the Lower Hunter Area Command and Maitland, nearly 60 kilometres inland to the west, is where the detectives reside for that Command.

On that day, however, the detectives, based on intelligence, had gone to the small town of Telarah, just west of Maitland, to execute a search warrant on a property suspected of housing drugs. The search had been planned for some time and needed the full resources of the detectives' unit, which meant that every available detective was at the search scene.

After police had made entry and had begun executing their warrant, one of the detectives at the search site, Detective Sergeant Peter Fox, received a call from the station officer at Maitland. The officer told him that the ambulance service had reported a man running around Clonmeen Circuit in Anna Bay covered in blood, screaming that his wife had been seriously injured and acting in a threatening manner. That was as much information as anyone had at the time. Peter, or Foxy as he is known to his colleagues, approached his manager, Detective Chief Inspector Rod Baker, and explained the situation. As much as Peter was needed on the search, a possible serious assault or murder takes precedence so he was forced to excuse himself. He grabbed fellow detective Graeme Parker and the two officers readied themselves to make their way to Anna Bay. Just before they left Peter addressed the remaining detectives and asked that when they concluded their search that they made their way to Clonmeen Circuit. If it were to become a murder inquiry more than two detectives would be needed to coordinate the investigation.

Even under lights and siren, the 60-kilometre drive to Anna Bay took close to an hour as the road conditions proved treacherous. The day had been grey and overcast, but the rain fell only intermittently and the falls weren't heavy enough to wash away the grease and oil from the road. Instead, the light rain only made driving conditions more hazardous, lifting the oil and creating a slippery smear across the bitumen. Being a Friday afternoon didn't help Peter Fox and Graeme Parker either, as they also had to battle the start of peak hour and weekend trekkers getting an early start. It seemed everyone was headed in the direction of Anna Bay.

Peter and Graeme kept a close ear on the police radio to listen for any further developments from Clonmeen Circuit. It wasn't long before they heard a uniform unit from Nelson Bay call off at the scene. The uniformed officers were Alec Cox, Craig Hall, and Greg Billingham. Peter immediately grabbed the radio and requested an update on the situation.

A little while passed before Alec Cox came back over the airwaves. The scene was confused and chaotic. Alec explained that a female was lying in a pool of blood in the entrance to her home and there was no knowing whether she was injured or dead as her husband was acting uncontrollably, attempting to access the house and preventing ambulance and police from doing their duties.

'Tell him it's a crime scene and he can't,' Peter ordered.

For Alec, that was easier said than done. Ross Brown continued shouting and being aggressive towards police and the ambulance officers. Eventually, the paramedics were able to get inside. Despite the extent of Judith's injuries, they checked for vital signs, as their training directed. They quickly realised there was no possibility of resuscitation: Judith was dead.

As the fracas continued outside, it was noticed that Ross had sustained a cut to the back of his left hand. A neighbour had earlier loosely wrapped the hand with a towel to try to contain the bleeding, but Ross discarded the makeshift bandage at the front door of his house. The reason for the cut was unknown to the officers at the time as Ross refused to give any explanation. Trying to calm the emotionally volatile Ross, the ambulance officers attempted to look at the wound, but their attention only increased his violent rage, resulting in one of the paramedics being punched in the chest.

When Peter and Graeme arrived in Clonmeen Circuit the entrance to the street was packed with people drawn by the sirens of emergency vehicles and Ross's screaming. It was also obvious that the relationship between Ross and the police had not improved. Alec and Ross were standing on the front lawn, with Alec still attempting to reason with the distraught husband and prevent him from entering the house. Ross waved his arms about and shouted abuse at the uniformed officer. Alec kept telling Ross that there was no way he could go inside, however much he protested. Ross appeared to accept the situation, if grudgingly, and paced back and forth across the lawn, which gave Alec a moment to quickly brief Peter, who had begun walking up the driveway.

Unlike television police shows, in which the informing police officer seems to know all about the victim and the circumstances surrounding the crime, then conveys the information in great detail, the reality is very different. The officers who arrive at a crime scene first have the job of preserving the scene, making sure onlookers are kept well away and that no one, including grieving relatives, does anything that may contaminate or compromise possible evidence that will later be collected by specialist police.

On this day, however, Alec and the other uniformed officers were having problems securing the scene, as their attention was taken up dealing with Ross's erratic behaviour.

When Alec met up with Peter he kept his appraisal of the situation short, while keeping one eye on Ross. 'This guy's wife's inside. She's dead. We don't know how. She could have slipped, or whether there's more to it … there's a lot of blood.'

Although Alec rightly left his options open as to the circumstances involved in Judith's death, Peter understood that Alec didn't accept that it was an accident. The emphasis Alec gave when he said 'there's a lot of blood' indicated to Peter that he was most likely dealing with a suspicious death.

Peter stood at the doorway and looked into the foyer where Judith lay. Her body was approximately one and a half metres in from where he stood. He saw what Alec had meant and made a cursory examination. The amount of blood covering the floor appeared greater than if Judith had just fallen and hit her head. He told Alec that no one was to enter the house and to secure the scene for forensics. The first rule in investigating a suspicious death is, 'Never go in'. The scene is the preserve of forensics, who wear special protective footwear and overalls so as not to contaminate the evidence.

Just as Alec had finished his brief assessment, Ross, predictably, made a move towards the house. Alec and Peter raced to stop him; Ross protested again, 'It's my fucking wife and I'm goin' in'.

Peter, who stands over 189 centimetres, put himself between Ross and the house and introduced himself, momentarily distracting Ross. As Alec had tried before, Peter attempted to placate Ross, explaining, 'We're trying to help you here. You'll be helping us by not going back in.'

Ross simply had one thing in mind: to get back into the house. He stood up close to Peter, just a few centimetres separating them, and shouted, 'You're not fucking telling me what to do. It's my fucking wife and I'm goin' back in. I want to see my wife!'

When Peter asked Ross to calm down, he responded with, 'I'll give you fuckin' calm down. I am angry mate. If you think I am angry now, you haven't seen anythin' yet'.

Ross's spittle sprayed over Peter's face. It was obvious to Peter that Ross was heavily intoxicated, which was very likely fuelling his rage and making it increasingly difficult to reason with him. As Peter stood his ground Ross continued his tirade, refusing to accept any directions from the police. Peter and the other officers bore the brunt of Ross's anger. It was as though Ross was trying to goad police into taking action against him, taunting them to see how far he could go before being physically restrained and arrested. At least that's how it seemed to the officers at the scene. Whether Ross was grieving and venting his anger at his wife's death, or whether he was intentionally baiting the police, the fact was Ross's behaviour was getting out of control and frustrating the investigation. Something had to be done.

Peter wasn't too sure what to make of Ross and his outbursts. 'Here's a man covered in blood. Why? His left hand is cut and bleeding. How did that happen? Is there more to it?

'At that time we [police] didn't know much and Ross wasn't giving us anything.'

In any homicide investigation those close to the victim, particularly the spouse, must be considered suspects until such time as evidence is presented to either confirm initial suspicions or eliminate them from the police inquiry. In fact, 80 per cent of homicides are committed by people known to the victim. Peter observed Ross's bizarre behaviour, not knowing if he was dealing with a possible murderer or just an overly emotional grieving husband.

Whatever the case, the last thing Peter wanted to do was arrest Ross, however disruptive he was being. 'Here's a guy who's come home and found his wife dead in the foyer of their home – how insensitive would that be [to arrest him]?'

There were moments when Ross would stop his outbursts and appear calm. Peter took advantage and tried to extract information, such as Ross's full name, where he had been that day, if Judith worked or stayed at home, and whether they had any children. He tried to gather small details to understand more about Ross, his relationship with Judith and the Brown family. Peter was able to gather from Ross that he had taken one of his boys to school a little after 8.00 a.m. and returned home to do some housework. The last time Ross saw Judith was at 9.00 a.m., when he left for the beach to walk his dog. Judith would normally leave for work between 9.15 and 9.20 a.m. Ross went straight to the Anna Bay Tavern after walking his dog and stayed there until the afternoon, when he returned home and found his wife's body.

Unfortunately, the periods of calm didn't last long and when they ended Ross would stride across the lawn and resume shouting abuse at police. This time he demanded his three boys be brought to the house.

'Ross, your wife's dead in there. You don't want your kids brought here,' Peter tried to explain, to no avail.

Ross only became angrier and repeated his demands. It was a ridiculous request and there was no way Peter was going to submit to it. The emergency vehicles and personnel surrounding the Browns' house would have been enough to traumatise the children, without risking what might happen if they chanced to see their mother lying bloodied in the foyer. Peter assured Ross that he would have the children collected and cared for and Ross could join them later. Peter's refusal only ignited Ross's fury, releasing another barrage of abuse at police.

Peter's patience and that of his colleagues was wearing thin. They had wasted enough of their energies trying to reason with Ross. Now it was time for drastic action. Peter turned to Alec and instructed him to arrest Ross. Legally, they had the right. Ross's behaviour was hampering their investigation and he had used offensive language. Peter didn't care what the charge was, he just wanted Ross out of the way.

It is not known if Ross overheard Peter and Alec talking, but his demeanour quickly improved as the officers approached. He became cooperative and accepted Peter's directive to sit in the police car and to wait for uniformed police to take him to Nelson Bay Police Station.

It wasn't the best start to an investigation, but now Ross was cooperating and some semblance of order had been restored. Peter went through his checklist, making sure all the appropriate people were contacted, such as the Homicide Unit, Forensics, Crime Scene and the local pathologist. He contacted his supervisor, Chief Inspector Rod Baker, and filled in him on the situation. There were also calls made to try to round up as many officers, preferably detectives, as soon as possible to help canvass the area for witnesses and assist the investigation where needed. If Judith's death was murder, and a weapon had possibly been discarded away from the house, a search of adjoining bushland would have to be conducted. At that moment there were only Peter and Graeme.

～

Reinforcements soon arrived in the form of two detectives, Inspector Geoff Leonard and Sergeant Kel Platt from the centralised Crime Agencies Homicide and Serial Offenders Unit. They were currently conducting investigations into the double murder of two women in the suburbs of Newcastle. Crime Agencies, based in Sydney, is a specialist division whose detectives are sent to locations around the state to assist and/or lead local detectives in investigations involving homicide, sexual assaults, organised crime and other serious offences.

Geoff and Kel were part of Strike Force Raphoe, formed a few weeks earlier after the bodies of Susan Kay, 33, and Joanne Teterin, 37, were found in Ms Teterin's Carrington home on 17 May. Both women had been bludgeoned to death. Police had established that the murders had been committed a week earlier, between 8.00 a.m. and 1.00 p.m. on 11 May. Then, on 30 May, 51 year old Robyn Denham's body was found in the bedroom of her Vine Street, Mayfield, home. She had been strangled with her stocking some time the previous night.

Because Judith's suspected murder occurred during daylight hours, as had Susan Kay and Joanne Teterin's, Geoff and Kel were curious to see if there were any similarities and if, perhaps, the same perpetrator had committed a third murder. They had already ruled out any connection between the murders of the two women and that of Robyn Denham. Inspecting the Clonmeen Circuit scene and assessing it against the double murder, Homicide detectives were satisfied that Judith's murder was not connected.

To help Peter, Geoff, and Kel went with a neighbour to intercept Ross's children before they reached

Clonmeen Circuit. Ross had told police that the two younger boys, Joel and Gene, would be walking home from school, while the eldest, Riley, would be on a bus. The neighbour arranged to take the boys to a house well away from the crime scene, and to wait there for the arrival of a counsellor from the Local Area Health Service. It would be left for the two Homicide detectives and the counsellor to break the horrific news to the boys. It was important that they find out from the children if there were any relatives or close family friends, someone from among people they knew well to give the boys emotional support and to make them comfortable, whom police could contact.

Inspector Rod Baker spoke with the boys that evening, later telling a curious media, 'We spent quite a bit of time with the boys … they're nice kids … they're holding up as good as could be expected … your heart really has to go out to these kids … I have three boys myself and I know how they'd feel if their mother went.'

⌐⌐

One of the most important aspects of the start of any investigation of a suspicious death is the identification and analysis of the physical evidence gathered at the scene. That evidence, however microscopic or seemingly insignificant at the time of its discovery, has the power to direct police enquiries and can even lead to a conviction. The art in crime scene examination is having the patience and focus to search for the evidence and the skill to identify what may be of importance.

According to Peter Fox, the Lower Hunter and Newcastle regions are blessed with some of the finest Crime Scene officers in the state. The eventual investigation surrounding Judith Brown's murder would put that statement to the test.

One of the Crime Scene examiners on duty that day was Detective Senior Constable Peter Muscio. Arriving at the scene, Peter donned gloves and shoe covers and conducted a cursory inspection to assess the situation and decide what support personnel and equipment he would need for a more detailed forensic study. Judith's body lay on her back; her head faced the front door. She was dressed in a red, white and blue horizontal striped casual top, blue slacks and runners.

The main bedroom, just off to the right of the house after walking along the foyer, had been ransacked; clothes and personal papers were scattered about. There were also bloodied shoeprints leading to the bedroom, and then to the sliding back door that led to a patio with a pergola. Peter took several Polaroid photos of Judith's body and of the scene for the benefit of Peter Fox and Graeme Parker. This would be the only way the two detectives would get to closely view Judith's body in the house without the risk of contaminating the evidence. Judith's face was bloated, bloodied and cut. It was obvious that the injuries could not have been caused by just a fall and, although the pathologist would be the one to determine the actual cause of death, it was clear that Judith was a victim of a serious assault. Peter Fox had a murder on his hands.

Knowing about the clothing and papers found in the bedroom, the bloodied footprints, the injuries suffered by Judith, and other findings would help Peter Fox and Graeme Parker when interviewing Ross Brown. Peter needed to know about Judith's daily routine, Ross's movements that day, and what Ross did when he discovered his wife's body, in the hope that these events might explain some of the physical evidence. The more Peter knew about the Browns, the quicker police could establish if this was an intended murder or if Judith was a victim of a botched break-in.

Having shown the Polaroids to Peter and Graeme, and deciding what other resources he required, Peter Muscio then needed to phone his supervisor. Unfortunately, he had problems getting a mobile signal and had to drive a few kilometres outside Anna Bay to find better coverage. Even police experience mobile phone problems.

A local lad and an industrial chemist with BHP, Peter Muscio decided to leave the steel manufacturer after the dramatic downturn and massive retrenchments throughout the steel industry during the 1980s. Although Peter was kept on by BHP, his future prospects were limited, so he decided to swap metallurgy for forensics and joined the New South Wales Police and served his probationary period at Maitland Police Station in 1988. During 1991 a Crime Scene Unit was established at the station and Peter was assigned the position of a leave assist, temporary officer, soon becoming a permanent member of the team in

1993. He quickly learned what the job was about when, having been with Crime Scene for only a few months, he was called to a fire at a hostel where twelve people had been burnt alive.

'It opened my eyes,' Peter admits. 'I found it intriguing. Challenging. And to identify each body as a person, which then allowed the families to have closure is very satisfying.'

In February 2000, four months before Judith Brown was murdered, Peter was involved in another case that would test his skills. It was one of Australia's most horrendous, cannibalistic murders that took place in the small Hunter Valley town of Aberdeen. Katherine Knight, an abattoir worker, stabbed her de facto, John Price, thirty-seven times. The day before his death Price had contacted police and taken out an Apprehended Violence Order (AVO) against Knight. After killing Price, Knight very skilfully skinned him, hung his pelt on a hook to dry, dissected the meat to make steaks, proceeded then to cook the meat with vegetables and gravy, boiled his head in a pot to make soup, and served his cooked flesh as a meal to two of his children. Knight was sentenced to life in prison and was the first female in Australia's criminal history to have her file marked 'Never to be released'. It was a crime scene that affected the most hardened of police.

~

Speaking with his supervisor from just outside Anna Bay, Peter Muscio requested the support of a fingerprints officer, the Video Unit, and another officer,

Detective Sergeant David Hancock, skilled in the art of photogramatry. Photogramatry produces 3D images using stereo cameras mounted on a tripod. The result enables police to accurately measure and plot distances, such as blood splatters from the body found on walls and objects, directly from the photographs created by this two-camera system.

Peter Muscio and the other officers needed to do their jobs first before the forensic pathologist would be called to attend the scene. There was little point in the pathologist turning up at that time, as it could be a long wait before the doctor would be allowed to see the body. Peter arranged to call the pathologist when all the Crime Scene officers had completed their tasks.

Fingerprint specialist Detective Senior Constable John Evans and Detective Senior Constable Gordon Miller from the Video Unit were dispatched to Clonmeen Circuit. Peter Muscio also asked for an additional Crime Scene examiner, but none were on hand. Peter, like Peter Fox, had to make do with what resources were available.

~

By late that winter's afternoon, when the sun was quickly setting, additional police had arrived in Clonmeen Circuit, including Chief Inspector Rod Baker. Peter Fox instructed detectives to begin speaking with neighbours, while uniformed officers kept onlookers and the growing media presence at a distance. Unlike in popular crime shows, Clonmeen Circuit was not filled with police cars and scores of police. The reality was that Peter Fox and Graeme Parker had only a handful of detectives to assist with the tasks that needed to be done. One advantage Peter believed he had was having the Homicide detectives on hand. Peter would take full advantage of their expertise as the circumstances surrounding Judith's death and the physical evidence became known. He would consult with Geoff Leonard and Kel Platt and use their experience as a guide to the investigation.

On Peter Muscio's return, he and the other Crime Scene officers dressed themselves in full protective overalls and began their examinations of the house. Between them, Peter and John Evans coordinated the control of the scene.

With the Crime Scene examiners now in control and other police canvassing the area for witness statements, it was a good opportunity for Peter Fox and Graeme Parker to have a lengthy, more intimate talk with Ross Brown. After all, there were a lot of answers the detectives needed before deciding what course the investigation would follow.

Before the uniformed police left with Ross, he was asked to open the garage door, which had a connecting door that led to the living area of the house. It was also where Ross had confined his dog, which was barking at all the commotion. Police didn't want to take the chance of being bitten or have the animal contaminate the scene any further, so they asked Ross to restrain his dog, Floyd. When Ross opened the garage the terrier darted out, excited, and ran around uncontrollably. It was clear that the dog was confused by all the people and attention being given to the house. Ross called to Floyd and lifted him onto the tray of the ute, tying him down so he couldn't jump out.

Peter Muscio checked the windows and doors from the outside; they showed no sign of forced entry, which meant either Judith knew her attacker or the perpetrator had gained entry through an open door, an unlocked window, or by deception. The main bedroom, where Judith and Ross slept, appeared to be in disarray. The wardrobe and drawers had been opened and clothes placed on the floor and across the bed, as were personal papers, bank statements, and the like. John Evans carefully bagged the papers for a detailed fingerprint analysis, which would be carried out later. A jewellery box had been tipped upside down and its contents spread over the dresser. The other bedrooms appeared to have been left undisturbed; all the beds in the house were made. The police noted that the remainder of the house was exceptionally clean and tidy. A basket of wet washing was found on top of the washing machine in the laundry, while a second clothesbasket contained a nightie and a grey flannel shirt, which were both damp.

Judith's body lay on the tiles in the entrance area, with her legs, from the thighs down, stretched over the carpet where the living–dining area began. The tiled section was drenched in blood and broken glass fragments from the two beer bottles Ross had dropped when he entered the house were scattered about. Peter

Muscio noticed that Judith's right forearm had a number of small cuts and very small slivers of beer glass adhered to the skin.

The liquid from the bottles had spread the blood across the foyer towards the front door. Ross had also dropped his glasses and set of keys by his wife's body, presumably when he bent down to cradle her. A dining chair had fallen on its side near Judith's feet and a packed lunchbox was found on the dining table itself. Blood splatters covered the walls and were also found on a narrow, waist-high, brick divide that separated the foyer from the main living–dining area. A circular blood impression was located on top of this partition, most likely caused by a cylindrical-shaped object that had come into contact with the blood and was then placed on the divide.

Bloodied shoeprints led away from Judith's body and across the carpeted area to the main bedroom. On closer examination a broken fragment of ceramic was found just inside the bedroom doorway. It was glued to the carpet with dried blood. As Peter Muscio bent down to examine the fragment more closely, he noticed what appeared to be fine slivers of glass mixed in with the blood.

Bloodied footprints, along with small, fading bloodprints that appeared to be the paws of Ross's dog, which led to the kitchen and the rear sliding door, were also found. The prints returned, fading as they trailed through the living–dining area to the sliding door giving access to the garage. Further shoeprints, which took the same path as the dog across the carpet to the garage, were found. Following the foot and pawprints Peter Muscio used Leuco Crystal Violet (LCV) to look for any bloodstains invisible to the human eye, particularly any that might be in the garage. This was important because, while police knew Ross had entered the house and locked his dog in the garage, there was no way of knowing exactly if all the footprints belonged to Ross or whether some could have belonged to Judith's assailant. Comparisons would need to be made against Ross's shoes.

LCV is used when bloody footwear impressions are visually located or otherwise suspected at a crime scene. LCV mixed with hydrogen peroxide reacts with the haemoglobin in blood, turning to a purple/violet colour on contact. The reaction can be viewed in normal light. LCV is also more sensitive than previous methods, providing a quick and uncomplicated technique of visualising and enhancing bloodstain impressions. As expected, the LCV revealed a trail of bloodied pawprints leading to the garage, but no footprints.

Peter conducted a cursory inspection of Ross's vehicle. There were bloodstains present, in particular one distinct bloodstain, found on the tray of the ute. It appeared to be a pawprint, which wasn't surprising, given that Ross's dog had blood on his paws. Another discovery did seem surprising and that was finding what appeared to be blood on the leather cover of the gearshift. At this stage, police did not know if Ross had, for any reason, accessed the cabin of his vehicle after finding his wife's battered body. When police first went to access Ross's Toyota HiLux they found the cabin door had been locked and were forced to break in. It seemed odd to police that Ross, after discovering his wife and given his erratic behaviour, would have entered the four-wheel-drive and then locked the vehicle. That issue would be left for Peter Fox to ascertain during his interview with the grieving husband. Peter Muscio would later have Ross and Judith's vehicles towed to Maitland Police Station for further study.

A closer examination of Judith's body revealed just how savage the beating she endured must have been. While an autopsy would comprehensively conclude what the injuries suffered by Judith were and suggest what weapon had been used against her, Peter Muscio's findings indicated that Judith had been beaten with a heavy object. Her face had suffered massive injuries to the right side, particularly to the forehead and scalp, which had a gaping wound and fragments of skull exposed. The left side of her scalp revealed a large gash, along with cuts, swelling, and obvious bruising. Her hands, raised above her head with the fingers curled, were also badly cut and swollen, and all her rings had been damaged. These injuries told police that Judith had tried in vain to protect herself from the vicious attack. As a matter of procedure, Peter placed plastic bags over Judith's hands to protect any evidence that could be found under the fingernails.

There was something else. Judith's watch had been broken. The glass or plastic casing was missing, the second hand was bent, and blood had congealed over the cracked face. The watch had stopped at precisely 9.14.28. More work would have to be done to know if the watch had stopped due to the attack, but if it had, then police would probably have an accurate time for Judith's murder. The watch would be left on Judith's wrist. It would not be removed until the time of the autopsy.

By 8.30 that night, Peter Muscio and the team were getting close to finishing their initial examinations. Peter spoke to the on-call forensic pathologist, Dr Tim Lyons, and informed him that the scene was available for him to examine. He let Dr Lyons know that he had tagged specific areas of interest: the blood spatters across the wall and the brick partition, areas where shards of glass had landed after the beer bottles had been dropped, the piece of ceramic in the main bedroom, and the staining from shoe and pawprints on the carpet. Peter would leave the scene tagged, ready for the next day when he would go over it all again and begin collecting samples, including DNA swabs, and removing a large part of the carpet for further analysis, separating out Ross Brown's shoeprints with any others that might have been present.

Chapter 2

9.14 P.M.

Arriving at Nelson Bay Police Station, Peter Fox and Graeme Parker wanted first to have Ross Brown's cut seen to by a doctor. The cut was deep and still bleeding; it would require stitches. The bandaging the paramedics applied to the left hand was only a temporary measure. Peter and Graeme took Ross to the Nelson Bay Polyclinic. While waiting for medical attention, they used the time to engage in small talk with Ross to try to gain his trust. If they were to find who had killed his wife, they needed Ross to have faith in them and to be candid in what he said. For all Peter and Graeme knew, Judith might have been a victim of a friendship or business association gone wrong: maybe even of someone out to get Ross. And there was still nothing at this early stage to say Ross wasn't involved. Police have to assume all possibilities, working from a broad base, until eventually, through the process of elimination, the investigation narrows.

During their time together, Ross explained that he and his family had moved to Anna Bay from the coal mining town of Singleton in the Upper Hunter only six months earlier. Most of Ross and Judith's close friends still resided in the northern town. Judith's parents,

Arthur and Elfrieda, lived in Queensland. Ross provided a list of names of family friends and relatives. Peter then organised for officers to make contact.

Among those contacted police spoke with two friends of Judith's, Murray and Sally (not their real names). Judith and Sally had struck up a close bond due to the fact that both their parents were German immigrants. They lived only a short distance from each other when the Browns were in Singleton, and their children would often have sleepovers, alternating between the two homes. Hearing the tragic news, Murray and Sally agreed to come down and support Ross and his children. Murray would meet up with Ross at Nelson Bay Police Station, while Sally went to be with the children. Ross's stepmother, Paula, was also contacted.

Police were to learn that Ross and his stepmother hadn't spoken for years. Whatever the reason for their estranged relationship, Ross, an only child, wanted Paula to be with him. His biological mother had died of natural causes when he was an infant and his father had remarried some eight to ten months later. Paula and Ross's father never had any children of their own. Ross's father died in the early 1990s. For Ross, Paula was the only mother he had ever known and Ross was her only child. Despite their differences, Paula drove to Nelson Bay to be with her stepson.

When a nurse came to assess Ross's injury, Peter and Graeme observed Ross's demeanour change. He went from being cordial to abusive and refused any medical help from the nurse. He hurled expletives at the health worker and adopted a persona of toughness, telling all who could hear that, 'My grandfather was a miner, my father was a miner, and I'm a fuckin' miner and we're fuckin' tough'.

As other nurses came to assist, Ross continued his tirade, threatening the staff if any one of them touched him. This resulted in one of the nurses almost walking out, even though Peter and Graeme were standing there ready to restrain Ross should he become physical. The two detectives were concerned that Ross would lose it.

The situation seemed, as it had been when police turned up to Clonmeen Circuit, impossible, that is, until a doctor arrived. It was explained to Ross that he would need two injections, a tetanus shot to counter any possible infection and an anaesthetic so his cut could be sutured. This news wasn't well received. Ross kept pulling his hand away. He told the doctor, 'You're not puttin' that fuckin' thing in me.'

The doctor used his best bedside manner, speaking calmly and putting his reluctant patient at ease.

With Ross's left hand now sporting ten stitches Peter and Graeme took him to Nelson Bay Police Station. Ross was first photographed in the clothing he had been wearing that day, a green bomber jacket with an open cut mining company logo, jeans, and runners. Once the police photographer was finished, Ross removed his clothes and shoes. They were placed in evidence bags and would be forensically examined. Police had arranged other clothing for Ross to wear to the interview.

The examination of the clothing would be done as a matter of course. Peter and Graeme didn't believe they'd extract any incriminating evidence from it as Ross had stated he cradled his wife. Whether intentional or not, Ross had a good excuse for having his wife's blood on his clothing, so police could not use this evidence against him.

By this time, Murray, the family friend from Singleton, had arrived at the station with his wife Sally. They were both shocked by the news of Judith's death, almost in disbelief. Together they offered Ross their support and condolences. Ross, who had agreed to take part in the interview, requested that Murray be present in the room. Peter and Graeme had no objection; they wanted Ross to be as comfortable as he could be under the circumstances. As the two men were led to the interview room, Sally was taken to where the three boys were being kept.

At 9.14 p.m., twelve hours after the estimated time of Judith's death, Peter Fox and Graeme Parker began an electronically recorded interview with Ross Brown. Ross and the detectives sat around a table, while Murray sat against the back wall, just behind his friend. At the start of the interview Ross's demeanour had changed markedly again. Although still having a hint of aggression in his voice he was more rational, cooperative, and sober in his responses. He gave the detectives a background on the family, how they'd lived in Singleton, had three children, and only recently moved to Anna Bay after Ross had accepted a voluntary redundancy. He repeated, calmly now, that he had worked as a driver in a coal mine and told them that he and Judith had sold their home before making the move. They were hoping to buy a new home in or around Anna Bay. Ross explained that he and Judith were happily married and they didn't have any financial worries. Ross didn't believe there was anything they owned in the house that was worth stealing or that would give anyone an excuse to kill Judith. He couldn't think of any reason why anyone would want to harm his wife.

Hearing Ross speak freely about his and Judith's past, Peter couldn't help but think that maybe Ross was just a grieving husband trying to cope with the situation. Ross had calmed down slightly and seemed in control. Peter had experienced similar angry reactions in people who weren't guilty of any crime. He knew that Ross's anger didn't mean he was any less sincere or full of grief than anyone else who had become hysterical and cried or refused to accept their loss.

But as the interview progressed, Ross's composure didn't last. He reverted back to his earlier aggressive, defensive manner, became short and irate, and almost threatened Peter and Graeme.

Several times Ross stood up and shouted at the detectives, 'You can go and get fucked … I'm walking out of here, I've had fuckin' enough …'

What sparked the tirade was Ross's frustration at being asked to give more detail of his movements for that day. They weren't accusing him of anything. All the detectives wanted to do was to be sure of where Ross was and the timeline he had given.

Ross explained that at about 8.15 that morning he took his eldest son, Riley, to Tomaree High School and arrived back home at approximately 8.30. The two younger boys left about ten or fifteen minutes later to walk to their school together. During this time the house was tidied up and a load of washing was taken out of the machine and placed in the basket to be hung out later. Judith prepared her lunch to take to work and she and Ross had a conversation before Ross left the house at 9.00 to take his dog, Floyd, for a walk along Birubi Beach. He proudly informed the detectives he had a pass to drive his Toyota four-wheel-drive along the beach to the sandhills, a popular location for visitors and locals alike.

In the interview Ross was insistent he left Clonmeen Circuit at 9.00 or maybe a little before. Peter challenged Ross on the preciseness of the time. After all, why didn't Ross stick around for another fifteen minutes to see his wife off? It was only fifteen minutes. Surely he could afford the extra time?

Peter couldn't understand why Ross hadn't hung around, as he admitted he wasn't bound by time because he wasn't working; nor did he have any appointments to keep. Ross stated he wanted to take his dog for a walk, repeating he left at or before 9.00. It was his routine. Judith would normally leave for the Salamander Childcare Centre between 9.15 and 9.20, to begin work at 9.30.

After letting his Staffordshire terrier run along the beach for an hour or more, Ross went straight to the

Anna Bay Tavern, arriving there at around 10.30. He remained at the Tavern drinking and speaking to a number of people he'd made acquaintances with since his arrival until some time between 1.30 and 2.00 p.m. As Ross prepared to leave he offered one of the patrons, Joe (not his real name), a lift home. Just as they drove away from the Anna Bay Tavern, Joe spotted someone he needed to speak with and Ross turned his vehicle around and drove back to the Tavern, where he remained for a short time. Joe bought him a beer, and then, while they were there, Ross used the opportunity to purchase two long-necked bottles of Toohey's New beer from the Tavern's bottle shop. Then he drove home, reaching Clonmeen Circuit at 2.40.

Immediately, he noticed his wife's car in the driveway. While he thought it was unusual, he just assumed Judith had become ill and decided not to go to work. He alighted from his vehicle, let his dog off the tray of the ute, and walked up to the front door carrying the two bottles of beer under one arm. He opened the door. The dog ran straight in and he followed. When he saw Judith lying on the floor he dropped the beer bottles and immediately cradled his wife, calling for her to 'Wake up, wake up'.

Ross told Peter, 'There's this fuckin' horrible thing … I didn't know if she was dead or not, all I knew there was fuckin' big trouble'.

Unsure as to what to do, Ross said he ran to Beth's house and asked her to call police. Peter asked why he requested police. Ross corrected himself and said he wasn't sure what he asked for, it could have been an ambulance. When asked about the cut to his hand, Ross was unsure how it had happened, and proceeded to point out other abrasions and cuts on his fingers. It was suspected that Ross received the cut by scraping the back of his hand against a shard of glass from the broken beer bottle, most likely when he reached under Judith's body to cradle her.

Peter was somewhat taken aback by the way Ross described finding his wife, especially his use of the phrase, 'this fuckin' horrible thing'. Ross and Judith had been married for around twenty years and he had already told police that he loved her and that they had had a good marriage. Yet, Peter kept hearing Ross speak of Judith in derogatory and depersonalised terms, such as referring to as 'thing' and 'that' when describing her bloodied body. It didn't ring true for Peter or Graeme that a loving husband would describe his wife in such a way. Ross's use of disparaging words might not have meant much and certainly didn't indicate any guilt, but it did cause Peter to take notice and wonder why.

A short break was taken just before the conclusion of the interview. In a special viewing room, Homicide detectives Geoff Leonard and Kel Platt watched the interview process. They'd arrived at the station shortly after its commencement, bringing along Ross's three boys and Sally. The Area Health Services counsellor and care workers from the Department of Community Services (DoCS) were looking after Sally and the children in a separate area of the police station.

During the break, Peter took the opportunity to consult with his Homicide colleagues. He wanted to know, from their experience if they had any questions they thought he should ask, if there was anything they thought he'd missed, and what their general impressions were. Peter, Graeme, Geoff, and Kel, the four detectives, conferred and bounced ideas off each other. It was felt that there was little more Peter and Graeme could have got out of Ross. Whether he was innocent or guilty, the interview had been thorough and would give the investigators a good base to work from, but it wasn't quite over yet.

When Peter and Graeme returned to resume the interview, Ross had become aware that his three boys were at the station, news that elicited another outburst when Ross demanded to see them straight away. Peter understood and accepted Ross's plea and offered to take him to see his kids, but explained to Ross that there were still a few questions that needed to be answered. Ross huffed and waved Peter's offer aside, sat down and said, 'Let's get this fuckin' thing over with first'.

Peter prefaced his final line of questioning with, 'Ross, I'm sorry, but I have to ask you some difficult questions … I have to ask this … Did you kill your wife?'

'You've got to be fuckin' kiddin,' Ross replied, which was followed by an emphatic, 'No!'

Did Ross have an argument with Judith that morning? 'No!'

Did Ross physically strike out at Judith for any reason that morning? 'No!'

Had Ross ever physically assaulted his wife? Again, 'No!'

It was all over. Peter wrapped up the interview. Ross had denied having anything to do with Judith's murder, so while he remained a suspect there was nothing Peter had that would cause him to arrest Ross that evening. In fact, Peter wasn't sure Ross had murdered his wife. Despite his behaviour and the way in which he referred to Judith, Peter felt he had just been dealing with a very angry, grieving husband.

There remained one last thing Peter needed Ross to do, and that was to take part in a walk-through. Peter asked Ross if he would be prepared to go back to the house and retrace his movements for the detectives. They wanted to know where he went, what he touched, and where the dog had been. This walk-through was necessary so they could compare Ross's movements against the physical evidence being collected by the Crime Scene examiners. Ross agreed to do it. The walk-through would be done some days later to give Ross time with his three boys and to try and settle down and get his life in order.

Now that the formalities were concluded Ross was reunited with his children.

Paula, Ross's stepmother, had arrived by this time. The Area Health Services and DoCS organised for a local motel to provide overnight accommodation for the Brown family and Murray and Sally. They would leave the next morning, where Ross and his children had organised to stay with Judith's brother in a western suburb of Newcastle.

~~~

It was near midnight. After seeing Ross and his family off, Peter and Graeme returned to Clonmeen Circuit. They had not finished working just yet. It's been stated in many a text, even referred to in television shows, that the first forty-eight hours of any murder investigation are the most important. The first twenty-four hours are usually the busiest: collecting potential forensic evidence, taking statements from possible witnesses while events are fresh in their minds, and making sure everything is done right. In Peter's words, 'Those first forty-eight hours are crucial. If you haven't honed in on possible suspects within that timeframe, then most times, the case can go unsolved.'

Walking around to the rear of the house, Peter and Graeme joined the other detectives and Crime Scene investigators who were gathered on the back patio under the pergola. It had been a long day, especially as most of the officers had been close to completing their shift when they were called to the scene. They were cold and hungry. Rain continued to drizzle, with the odd gust blowing up and spraying icy droplets around, creating an even greater chill in the air. Despite the conditions and their weariness, the officers were still alert, fuelled by adrenalin. Their interest heightened when they saw Peter and Graeme. Everyone was curious to know what Ross had to say, particularly as some police, especially those who had examined the scene, had theories to share.

For Peter and Graeme, the interview with Ross gave them information that they would need to check out. They would need to speak with Anna Bay Tavern patrons and collect any security footage to check against Ross's timings. From the point of view of timing, Ross's cut hand was a concern. If Ross was lying about when he received the cut, patrons at the Tavern should have been able to tell police if they remembered Ross having the injury that morning. It was also hoped that a neighbour might have seen Ross leaving the house and be able to give an accurate time, which again, would either support or refute his statement. Did Ross leave at 9.00 or later, and if later, by how much?

Did any of the neighbours see anyone suspicious in the street, or in the adjoining bushland? Had any of the neighbours noticed anyone acting suspiciously in the last few days? Had there been any reported break-ins in the area?

By this time Peter Muscio and John Evans had completed their initial scrutiny of the crime scene. Peter Muscio briefed Peter Fox on his observations from that evening. Although accurate conclusions could not be drawn until a detailed study of the evidence had been completed, there seemed to be no obvious evidence left behind by an intruder. The shoe impressions found on the carpet appeared to be of one type and, most likely, belonged to Ross, given their knowledge that he'd entered the house. There was also still the question of a murder weapon. Nothing that stood out as a weapon had been discovered in or around the immediate area of the house. Along with the broken piece of plaster found in the main bedroom, smaller, at times minute, pieces of ceramic had been found next to the body and near the front entrance. There was a lot of broken glass from the beer bottles, but it would be the pathologist's call to say what implement was most likely the weapon.

When Peter Fox and Graeme arrived, pathologist Tim Lyons was already conducting his examinations. He had arrived only a little earlier, at around 11.30 p.m. Judith's body still lay in the foyer. It is normal procedure that the body is not moved by anyone until the forensic pathologist arrives on the scene.

Of course, it isn't always the case that a forensic pathologist gets to visit the crime scene, particularly as the Hunter–New England Area Health Service Forensic Pathology Unit is responsible for homicide and suspicious deaths within the Hunter and northwestern regions of New South Wales. Attending a scene where possible, however, enables the pathologist to reconstruct the principal series of events that led to death. Looking at the disposition of the body, the injuries suffered by the victim, blood spatter patterns, and other evidence picked up by the Crime Scene examiners gives the pathologist the ability to paint a picture of the circumstances surrounding the victim's death. For Tim Lyons, being at the crime scene is crucial in being able to make this evaluation, which is invaluable when later examining the body and deciding what or how injuries were caused.

In Tim Lyons' words, 'You can only do that by being there and feeling and understanding the ambience of the scene and the environment … I think you have to actually be there and walk through [the scene and its surroundings] to have that three-dimensional image in your mind.

'It's a big problem covering a big area that you sometimes can't always get to the scene, so you're looking at two-dimensional pictures and looking at crime scene videos is not the same as being there and being able to view it properly and see the whole thing.'

Peter Fox was especially pleased to meet up with Tim Lyons. They had worked on cases before and Peter Fox had nothing but praise for Tim and his wealth of knowledge in the area of forensic pathology. In Peter Fox's opinion, having Peter Muscio there as well meant he couldn't have had two better professionals at the scene. He knew that, whatever their findings, their work would be thorough and meticulous. He trusted their assessment and was anxious to know what they had to say.

Born in the Cotswolds of England, Tim Lyons has received the highest qualfication in Surgery and has spent close to ten years as a surgeon, as well as a general practitioner. He's also an adventurer who teamed up with the Royal Geographical Society in Sarawak, Borneo, on caving expeditions, and joined a British Army expedition to the world's deepest cave in France. Tim worked for two years in Cape Town, South Africa, in the hectic and demanding surrounds of a trauma unit, before returning to England where he took up a post as an academic at Manchester University lecturing in anatomical pathology.

While indulging his love for teaching, Tim would often accompany a colleague, Bill Lawler, to crime scenes. Performing hospital and coronial post mortems became part of their routine workload. The exposure to forensic pathology soon developed into a passion for Tim, who found this unusual area of medicine very challenging and professionally satisfying.

Listening to Tim's precise English accent it is difficult to believe that he spent some time in Australia as a child. His father was an airline pilot and the Lyons family called Sydney home; Manly, to be precise, on the northern beaches. Even though the family returned to England, Tim promised himself he would find his way back some day. The Aussie sun, surf, sand, and lifestyle had seduced him.

In 1994 Tim noticed an advertisement in the *British Medical Journal* for a director of forensic pathology in Tasmania. So keen was Tim to apply that the night he called to register his application he almost missed the boat that had been booked to take him and his family on holidays. Not backwards in coming forwards, Tim told the contact on the advertisement that he wanted the job and for them not to give it to anyone else. They obviously listened, and Tim was appointed to the position the following year.

Settling down in the idyllic apple isle, Tim would

have hardly expected it to become the focus of an event that would create headlines across the world. On 28 April 1996, 28-year-old Martin Bryant went on a shooting rampage in and around the historic town of Port Arthur, located on the lower southeast coast of the state. He was eventually arrested after fleeing from a burning building he had been held up in, where he sporadically shot at police to keep them at bay. After an 18-hour standoff, Bryant had killed 35 people—men, women and children—and injured a further 53. It was the largest mass murder in Australia's history and it put Tasmania on the international crime stage.

Identifying the victims, their cause of death, and configuring a sequence of events to assist police with their prosecution tested Tim's skills and those of his team. During this time, Tim gratefully accepted support from technical and medical forensic experts from New South Wales and Victoria. But he believes his work was made easier by the professionalism of the Tasmanian police, who secured the crime scenes, and the other forensic pathologists, who worked tirelessly to find the answers.

A sad endnote to Port Arthur was a murder–suicide that involved five victims. Peter Shoobridge was a published poet who restored antique furniture. Some knew him as the 'Bush Poet'. Estranged from his wife, he was independently wealthy and lived with his four daughters in a large home just outside Hobart. One Sunday he slit the throats of his daughters, aged 9, 12, 14, and 18, and then took his own life with a .22-calibre rifle. Just before his suicide, Shoobridge posted letters to friends and relatives. As tragic as it was, Tim was moved even more by the apparent reason Shoobridge suggested in his letters was the motive for the killings. Shoobridge had decided he didn't want his girls growing up in a 'troubled world'. It was believed he was referring to the actions of Martin Bryant. Local media gave Shoobridge another nickname, the 'Tasmanian Devil'.

While living in Tasmania, Tim had joined the Australian Air Force Reserve. Because of his background as a pathologist he was asked to assist the air force in its examination into a fatal crash of an F-111 fighter jet, and also went overseas to New Guinea to assist in the recovery of recently discovered bodies of former Australian soldiers who had died there during World War Two.

In 2000 Tim and his family made the move north to Newcastle. Originally he wanted to get back to Sydney, but when the opportunity for Newcastle came up, Tim and his wife found they preferred the Hunter region and decided to make it their home.

People often ask Tim what he does as the director of forensic pathology. Their reactions are varied when he explains his work and just how busy his section is. There are many more suspicious, accidental, and unknown causes of deaths that need his department's services than are made public.

A short time after Tim's arrival to Newcastle, he was faced with one of the most gruesome killings he had ever experienced. It was the cannibalistic murder of

John Price by Katherine Knight at Aberdeen. Tim worked alongside Peter Muscio at the crime scene, and from that working relationship gained great respect for Peter's methodical approach to his work.

∾

Looking at Judith's body, Tim Lyons noticed the severity of the injuries she had suffered. The scene was bloodier than he had expected, mainly because the liquid from the beer bottles had mixed with the blood and spread it over a larger area. One of the questions the police had for Tim was whether the beer bottles could have been used as a weapon. Could they have caused the injuries? Small fragments of glass were strewn across the area, as though the bottles had exploded rather just been dropped. At least that was how Peter Fox saw it.

Peter had decided to view the scene for himself. Wearing shoe covers he trod carefully, entering from the connecting door to the garage to minimise any possible contamination. Peter was amazed at how busy the scene was. The actual foyer area was small, but there was so much debris and blood that it was, ironically, a big crime scene, which meant the Crime Scene examiners had to be especially meticulous in identifying and extracting the glass fragments and blood samples, and in recording the spatter patterns and any other evidence. Peter explained that finding a body with a knife in its back in a large field is actually a small crime scene compared to what they found in the Clonmeen Circuit house. It was no wonder Peter Muscio and his team would need several days to fully examine it.

Tim took a closer look at Judith's injuries and tried to decide if the police theory regarding the beer bottles as being the weapon had merit. He noticed the blood spattering across the wall and on the small partition. The spatter pattern was irregular. While the study of blood patterns is more the expert field of the police Crime Scene Unit, Tim's experience told him that the irregularity of the pattern indicated Judith had suffered more than one application of blunt force trauma: in other words, Judith had been struck several times. He also noticed a vague indentation in Judith's face that didn't appear consistent with an attack by a bottle.

Abrasions, cuts, and imprints left by different types of objects have certain characteristics. Had, say, a beer bottle been used to strike Judith, Tim would have expected to see a circular imprint, not the deep impression he was staring at. Crime scenes are complex, and Tim knew that there was still the possibility that Judith could have initially been struck with a bottle and another implement used later to finish the job. Whatever it was would not be known until the autopsy revealed just how much Judith had suffered at the hands of her aggressor. In Tim Lyons' opinion though, the beer bottles would not have caused the injuries. The damage was very significant and was probably caused by a heavier object than a full beer bottle. The weapon used would have been of considerable weight. Tim also believed that Judith sustained most of the injuries as she lay on the tiled foyer, very possibly rendered unconscious, or at least knocked to the ground and then set upon. Obviously, it was a very vicious attack.

The beer bottles were still of concern to Peter Fox. Given Ross's explanation of dropping the bottles, Peter expected the immediate scene around Judith's body to be littered with glass fragments. It was. There were a lot of glass shards in the foyer; when Peter entered from the garage door he found fragments near him on the carpet. Although it would have to be tested, Peter found it extraordinary to find glass that had sprayed such a distance, a good five metres or more, if the bottles had only been dropped. Not only that, but the glass would also have had to fly over the brick partition. Peter believed the bottles would surely have been thrown down with force to disperse the glass in the way they had.

On the wooden shelf of the partition there was a circular impression in blood; Peter was sure that the bottom of a beer bottle had left that mark. The circumference certainly matched. There were also faint ridges in the blood, again consistent with the bottom of a beer bottle. Peter Muscio was of the same opinion. If not, what could have been there? A vase? A round glass or metal coaster? If so, where was it and how did it manage to transfer blood to the shelf? Whatever the item, there was no question that it had been placed on the partition after Judith's murder. It would be a matter they'd need to put to Ross when they spoke to him during his walk-through.

There was also the matter of Judith's watch and that it had stopped at 9.14.28. While the second hand had been bent in the attack, it was possible to see that, if straightened, it pointed directly at the 28-second mark. Peter and Tim agreed that it is very rare that a broken watch found on a victim gives investigators the time of death. In fact, never in their careers had either experienced such a finding. That sort of luck is usually reserved for fictional detective stories.

Tim lectures on crime scene procedures to police and forensic personnel. He often warns his audience against trying to give an exact or narrow estimate of the time of death, as they do on television, because such a deduction is virtually impossible. It is also not helpful to an investigation which, as it progresses, may find evidence that can conflict with an established time. It is always better to give a broad timeframe and let the investigators try to determined the exact time of death from witnesses who last saw the victim or from the killer when in custody.

The exception to this is viewing a broken watch on the wrist of a victim of a bomb blast. Forensic experts in the United Kingdom found that from their experience they could estimate the time of death of victims of bomb attacks by when their watches had stopped. The watches ceased to work usually as a result of the blast or being damaged in the debris that resulted from it. Tim had never actually witnessed a broken watch being helpful at a murder scene.

Yet, here they were, and based on the statement from Ross, Judith would have left for work at about 9.15, so the time on her watch could actually be the time she tried to fend off the attack and died. Of course, Peter still had to consider if Judith's watch had been correctly set; it might have been running several minutes fast or slow. Some people deliberately set their watches ahead of the normal time in order not to be late for appointments. Other people neglect to replace batteries or service their watch and it can run slow.

Another possibility could be that whatever came in contact with the watch face could have moved the hands, a theory supported by the bent second hand. So, as much as Peter would have liked the watch to show him the time of death, the fact was there was no way of knowing exactly until a further study of the clockwork was conducted.

~

During the course of any investigation police must decide what they will release to the media that may help them find their killer, information that may prompt the memory of witnesses, or encourage those whom the killer has confided in to come forward. Likewise, the police must decide what evidence they need to hold back. In some cases the information held back can be used to eliminate those individuals who, for reasons known only to themselves, decide to admit to crimes they haven't committed. Therefore, any withheld evidence can also be used to identify the perpetrator, particularly if witnesses come forward with information that ties in with the evidence. Should Judith's watch prove to show the time of her murder, it would give police an accurate timeframe, so if witnesses identified a person or persons being around the Clonmeen Circuit house around 9.15 that morning, or a suspect did not have an alibi for that time, then police could focus on that individual.

That night Peter Fox made the decision that no one was to talk to the media about the watch. While Peter enjoyed a good working relationship with the local media, the information about the watch would be something he needed to keep close to his chest.

Peter Muscio was concerned about something. In all the years he had worked as a crime scene examiner, he'd never come across an attempted break-in where the belongings had been laid out in such an orderly fashion. The clothing from the wardrobe had been taken out in bundles and draped on the bed. Items from the drawers appeared to have been picked up in a clump and placed on top of the dresser. In his experience, perpetrators tend not to be so careful. Clothing is usually thrown out of the wardrobe one piece at a time, and drawers are pulled right out and the contents scattered about.

It also appeared, but would need to be checked with Ross, that nothing of value had been taken. The jewellery box had been opened and tipped over, but there was still jewellery there. It was also noted that no other room, other than the main bedroom, had been touched. Why had the offender, if an offender had broken in, and then killed Judith for whatever reason, seemingly not bothered to take anything, especially as it looked as if the perpetrator had been looking for something?

Having searched the house it became apparent to police that there was an item missing. On the dining table was Judith's packed lunch, as well as a plastic bag containing craft material. It was thought Judith had planned to take this material with her to work for the children to use. If Judith had collected everything she needed to take with her that morning and put it on the dining table, where was her purse? Police did not find Judith's purse, or anything resembling a purse or handbag, in any part of the house. Again, they'd need to check with Ross how Judith carried her money, credit cards, and identification.

Admittedly, the police were having their doubts about Ross's involvement, but while some of the evidence pointed to him, police weren't, as Peter Fox put it, 'putting all their eggs in one basket'.

Before Peter left that night he organised for volunteers from the local State Emergency Services and uniformed police officers to conduct a foot search of the immediate area in daylight hours. They would search the bushland area and neighbouring backyards, in the hope that they just might find the weapon used to kill Judith Brown.

At about 1.00 a.m. on Saturday 3 June, the government contractor arrived and removed Judith's body from the house. As they were lifting her, a small, circular piece of clear plastic fell on the tiled floor and bounced onto the carpet. It was the cover for Judith's watch. Police, who had been curious as to what had happened to the cover, retrieved it and placed it in an evidence bag.

The Clonmeen Circuit house was locked and secured. A uniformed police officer would stand guard until later that morning when Peter Fox, Graeme Parker, and Peter Muscio would all return to continue their investigation.

Chapter 3

KEEPING AN OPEN MIND

Peter Fox lived roughly an hour and half's drive away from Anna Bay. Having left the crime scene after 1.00 on Saturday morning, 3 June 2000, he caught a couple of hours' sleep, woke up, shaved, and bade his family farewell before heading straight to Nelson Bay Police Station. The story was the same for the other officers who were on site the previous evening.

Reaching Nelson Bay, Peter met up with Graeme Parker, Chief Inspector Rod Baker, and close to a dozen other detectives who had gathered for a briefing. As they went over the crime scene, it was obvious to all that it raised more questions than it gave answers. This situation energised Peter in particular. He didn't want to stop and needed to know more. There was a lot of work still to be done. Priorities were set in what the police needed to know first and what could wait for another time.

Peter began organising the detectives in teams and directing each team with tasks he wanted carried out that day. It was important that each detective keep a detailed running sheet of everything they did: who they spoke to, what they found, and if anything needed to be followed up. This is crucial for a homicide investigation. While police do their best to solve a murder quickly, sometimes that just doesn't happen. Should a case stretch into years, having detailed running sheets from the onset of an investigation can be of great help in solving it.

The teams were given their assignments. Peter tasked a fellow detective, Senior Constable Peter Wright, to check on Ross's statement that he had been at the Anna Bay Tavern from 10.30 a.m. until about 2.00 p.m. the previous day. Peter Wright would have to speak with staff and patrons, get their impressions of Ross's behaviour during the day and find out if anyone noticed Ross bearing any abrasions or cuts. Security footage from the Tavern would also be collected. This was the best way for police to compare the timings for when Ross arrived at the Tavern and when he departed.

Staff at the Tavern's bottle shop would be interviewed to see if they knew Ross and if they remembered him buying the two long-necked bottles of Toohey's New. Peter Fox had been told there was a second bottle shop further up the street, Abb's Bottle Shop. Staff at both shops knew Ross. Peter Fox asked Peter Wright to check there as well, just in case Ross had mistaken which bottle shop he'd made his purchase from. Cash register recipes for the Friday were taken from both bottle shops. They would be scrutinised to try to find the time of the transaction for the two bottles of beer.

Before Peter Wright set off, Peter Fox instructed him to set his watch to the exact time, then compare the time on his watch against the time shown on the security video and the sales receipts. It's been Peter Fox's experience that the times displayed don't always match the actual time. They can vary as little as only a couple of minutes, and in some cases can be as much as an hour out, due to the proprietors not re-setting the clocks after the beginning or end of daylight saving time. Peter Fox wasn't taking any chances: he wanted to be sure when Ross arrived at the Tavern, when he left, and when he made his purchases.

Whether Ross was the perpetrator or not didn't matter. Ross had given police a statement detailing the events leading up to the discovery of his wife's body. In any investigation police must verify what people tell them. The thoroughness of their enquiries can be helpful in proving a person's innocence as much as in revealing their guilt.

The next step for police was to find the alleged weapon. Peter Fox had already organised for a sweep of the bushland behind Clonmeen Circuit, which might ascertain whether the assailant or assailants dropped the weapon there in a rush to escape the scene. The other question remained: If Ross killed his wife, where would he have disposed of the weapon? With that in mind, Peter also directed detectives to Birubi Beach to search garbage bins and to look among the coastal rock formations and sand dunes.

Searching the sand dunes was a daunting task. The dunes, which run for 17 kilometres from Anna Bay to Stockton, the northern point of Newcastle harbour, are five to six kilometres wide. The sand dunes are a magnet for four-wheel-drive enthusiasts, mostly tourists, who spend the weekend testing their skills and their vehicles. Between natural wind erosion and the churning of the sands by weekend warriors, the sands have given up secrets from the past. Aboriginal skeletons dating back some six hundred years have been discovered along the stretch of sand. The question foremost in the detectives' minds was: where to start?

Another problem for detectives was that they didn't know what they were looking for. Peter couldn't be any more specific than to tell them it was a heavy object. It could have been anything—a mallet, a piece of metal, even a lump of concrete. The detectives would just have to keep their eyes open for anything that looked out of place or showed signs of carrying blood. It was all they had to go on.

Peter didn't want to waste time, and it wasn't long before all the detectives had dispersed and were conducting their individual enquiries. Four detectives remained at Nelson Bay Police Station taking detailed statements from all the neighbours. Peter, Graeme Parker, and Rod Baker returned to Clonmeen Circuit. They were met by ten Operational Support Group police and members of the State Emergency Services, dressed in their distinctive fluorescent orange overalls, all waiting for directions. They were split into small groups, some sent to search neighbouring backyards, while others were lined up side by side and walked slowly through the bushland looking for anything that might be connected to Judith's murder.

Inspector Baker addressed the media, who were anxious for updates. He could give them only vague responses, explaining that Judith had died from head injuries and that more details would not be known until after the autopsy. He asked for anyone with any information to contact the Crime Stoppers hotline or call the Nelson Bay Police Station. Journalists asked if Judith's death was the result of a botched break-in, but Rod Baker refused to be drawn. He simply replied, 'We're keeping an open mind.'

The media were naturally anxious to know if there was a link between Judith's murder and the murders of the other three women in the Newcastle area. Journalists even went so far as to measure the crime scenes and reported that they were all committed within a 60-kilometre radius. Peter Fox fielded the question and told Sasha Westwood from Sydney's *Daily Telegraph*, 'We have nothing to indicate there is a link … it's unusual [to have four murders], but we're not attaching anything special to it … of course, we'll explore it, but we don't have anything to link them.'

Peter was quick to quash any suggestion that, as the media put it, a 'madman was on the loose', repeating they had not found any link between the murders and, 'We don't want to alarm the public'.

To explain why Homicide detectives Geoff Leonard and Kel Platt had visited the Clonmeen Circuit crime scene, Peter said, 'They were here assisting us, offering expert advice, but at this stage we're not treating the deaths as a serial'.

While the police and volunteers were conducting a search outside, Peter Muscio was back at work inside the house. He began taking samples of the blood found on the handles of the rear sliding doors, the walls, and the partition, and carefully removed the blood-glued piece of ceramic found in the main bedroom. He found other, smaller pieces of ceramic and cement grit near where Judith's body had lain and just inside the entrance doorway. Large sections of carpet from throughout the living–dining area and the main bedroom were sliced and removed for closer examination.

The shards of glass from the broken beer bottles were collected. Peter found two bottle tops, two bases, and enough glass that, when weighed, would equate closely to there having been two bottles broken at the scene. The bottles were too shattered to be put back together. Peter also removed every bloodstained tile from the foyer area. He would carry out a lengthy and meticulous study of the crime scene and the entire house from the Friday afternoon through to the following Wednesday.

At Nelson Bay Police Station numerous neighbours filed in to assist police by giving their statements. Other than finding anyone who may have seen anything suspicious, it was important for police to be aware of what the neighbours knew about Ross and Judith. Were the Browns happily married, as Ross would have police believe? Did they argue? Were there regular visitors to the house? If so, did anyone know who they were?

All the neighbours seemed to agree that Ross and Judith Brown were a happy couple, an average family by all accounts. No one could remember ever hearing any arguments. Admittedly, not everyone knew the Browns well, but what the neighbours did know supported what Ross had told police. Unfortunately for the investigators, no one saw anything or anyone suspicious in the street.

Some neighbours did notice Judith's car in the driveway. They thought it unusual, as they all knew that Judith worked at the Salamander Child Care Centre. Some remembered seeing the Browns' two younger children leaving for school at around 8.40 a.m. As for Ross's movements that morning, no one could say for sure when he left the house. It seemed none of the statements could be used to confirm or reject Ross's statement that he left at 9.00 a.m.

Several neighbours commented on the weather that Friday morning. They stated that it was raining and windy.

While most of the neighbours didn't give police any details relating to the murder, one, Tina, did have some interesting information. Tina was the woman who, along with Beth, had broken away from Ross's grip as he had attempted to drag her into the house to see Judith's body.

In her statement to police Tina stated that at about 11.00 a.m. on the Friday one of Judith's co-workers from the childcare centre called at her door. The co-worker told Tina she was trying to find out why Judith wasn't at work. Judith hadn't phoned the centre to say she was sick. Seeing Judith's car in the driveway, the co-worker had knocked on her door and called out her name. Judith hadn't responded. The co-worker asked Tina to accompany her back to Judith's house. Music could be heard coming from a radio inside the house. The two women walked around to the back of the house where they found the rear sliding door was unlocked. The co-worked pulled the door open slightly and called Judith's name. Again, there was no response. The co-worker wanted to walk in, but Tina stopped her. Tina explained that she convinced the co-worker that she didn't know Judith very well and felt uncomfortable walking in on her. The co-worker accepted Tina's reluctance, and then left. Tina returned home and didn't hear anything more until Ross arrived home and began screaming and shouting up and down the street.

Police were unable to speak to anyone from Judith's work until it reopened for business on the Monday. They found out that on the day of the murder Judith's manager from the childcare centre phoned her home at 9.55 a.m. Judith was usually punctual, so staff at the centre were concerned that they hadn't heard from her. After the co-worker's visit to Clonmeen Circuit, staff at the centre began calling again in the afternoon. The calls were unanswered.

There was one question police put to both Tina and Judith's co-worker that was of great interest. Had they noticed any liquid, be it blood or other, seeping from under the front door of the house when they were there in the morning? Neither woman had noticed any liquid. This was important to the investigators, because when Peter and Graeme arrived at the scene that afternoon, blood was coming out from under the front door. The amount of beer from the two bottles Ross had broken caused the blood to travel. As the women didn't notice this in the morning, it meant Ross's story that he had dropped the bottles in the afternoon on his return home was possibly verified.

Peter Fox couldn't help but wonder 'What if?' when he read Tina's statement. Had the women entered the house at that time, would police have had better evidence to point to a suspect? Would they have been closer to making an arrest at this early stage? Whatever Tina's reasons were for not walking into the house, the fact was she didn't, so Peter and his team had to deal with what they had—a disorganised and contaminated crime scene that was yielding very little evidence.

At the Anna Bay Tavern, Peter Wright struck a slight problem. One of the Tavern's windows had been kicked in by vandals some time between close of business on Thursday night and the early hours of Friday morning. Police who attended the incident had taken the security tapes, and new tapes weren't fitted until later on the Friday morning, after the time Ross claimed he had arrived. This meant police could not verify what time Ross began drinking, though they would know how long he had stayed.

Despite the hitch at the start, a quick look at the tapes did corroborate Ross's statement: they showed that Ross was at the Tavern until around 2.00 in the afternoon. He sat on a stool at a raised table in the bar area, dressed in the same clothing he was wearing at the time police answered the emergency call to Clonmeen Circuit. His clothes appeared clean.

While Ross drank, different patrons joined him at various times throughout the day. The tapes also revealed that Ross's left hand was free from any injuries. Again, the tapes showed Ross was telling the truth, that he had most likely cut his hand when reaching under Judith's body to cradle her.

Patrons knew Ross and remembered him drinking at the bar on the Friday. He didn't appear to them to be any different than usual. It seemed to be a routine for Ross to spend some time at the Anna Bay Tavern between doing the housework and being home for his children when they returned from school. However, there was a slight change in his routine on the Friday. Ross would normally call into the Tavern around lunchtime, have a couple of schooners of beer, and then leave. He would usually be at the Tavern for only an hour or two, but on the Friday he was there from 10.30 until some time after two o'clock.

The staff at the two bottle shops weren't sure whether they had seen Ross on the Friday afternoon or if they had sold him just two long-necked bottles of Toohey's New. The security videotapes and cash register recipes would need to be checked to find the sale.

Following Peter Fox's request, Peter Wright checked his watch against the Anna Bay Tavern Bottle Shop's security video and register receipts. Peter Fox was right. The time displayed on the security footage ran eight minutes fast, while the time shown of the cash receipts was a couple of minutes behind. The time shown on Abb's Bottle Shop's security vision was also running a few minutes late. Knowing this meant police could accurately marry the video with the receipts to show which people arrived at what time and what they purchased. At this stage Peter Fox didn't know if he would need to be so precise with this evidence. It was more a preparedness step, just in case the videos and receipts revealed any inconsistencies in Ross's statement.

After an extensive search of the bushland and neighbouring backyards in Clonmeen Circuit, nothing was uncovered that could be linked to the murder scene. Detectives exploring Birubi Beach, the garbage bins, the surf-washed rock faces and the Stockton sand dunes also came away without finding anything suspicious.

By the end of Saturday 3 June 2000, over twenty-four hours after the start of the investigation, Peter Fox and his team had no clear suspect or motive for the murder of Judith Brown. It was a frustrating situation for the investigators, but it was still early days. The autopsy had yet to be performed; results from the evidence collected by Peter Muscio, John Evans, and their team of examiners wouldn't be known for weeks. Peter Fox hoped that the findings at the autopsy and the forensic evidence would help narrow the investigation.

In any major investigation where a taskforce is formed, a name is assigned, as designated by NSW Police Headquarters in Sydney and relying on the progressive use of the alphabet. The homicide strike force established in Newcastle for the double murders of Susan Kay and Joanne Teterin was named Raphoe. The next letter in the alphabet is 'S', so Sydney gave Peter Fox and his team the code name Saltburn.

Some people questioned the appropriateness of the name. It was thought that the use of the word 'burn' was too harsh. A request was put to headquarters to change the designation. The request was accepted; the taskforce would be known as Saltpond.

For the residents of Anna Bay murders were normally unpleasant events that occurred in large cities such as Sydney or Newcastle, and were only ever brought to their attention through the media. To have a murder happen in the village-like, rural community filled locals with trepidation. Windows and doors were locked. Residents looked warily upon visitors to the area. The usually welcoming ambience of the Bay had changed.

Some of the neighbours in Clonmeen Circuit who had witnessed the events on the Friday afternoon were traumatised by the incident and spent sleepless nights wondering if the killer was still lurking around the area. It wasn't long before houses were put on the market so the owners could try to distance themselves from the tragedy and the nightmares it was causing them to have.

Geoff Robinson, a fifth-generation resident of the area, would speak with Jason Bartlett from the *Newcastle Herald* a year later on how the murder had transformed the town. 'I knew something was wrong by the speed with which the police cars raced past my office ... As soon as I saw the scientific vehicles I knew it was something more than an accident.

'It has placed increased awareness on the fact these horrendous crimes, and it certainly was a horrendous crime, can occur in a rural close-knit community ... We were certainly made aware very quickly of the need for increased security ... The habit of leaving doors unlocked was no longer part of the atmosphere.

'This just wasn't a place where murders occur, although it did in this case, it's just not what the area is about at all.'

Geoff Robinson concluded by saying, 'We just don't know who did this and why it was done ... That's a concern shared by many in the community, that a life can be taken for no apparent reason.'

Chapter 4

PERSONS OF INTEREST

On Sunday 4 June, Peter Fox, in the company of Peter Birch, another detective from the taskforce, attended Judith Brown's autopsy at the John Hunter Hospital's morgue in Newcastle. Peter Muscio was also there and collected Judith's clothing, her shoes, the rings from her fingers that had been dented in the attack, and the watch. Scrapings were collected from under Judith's fingernails, as well a blood samples; strands of hair were found resting in Judith's palms. Peter would examine the clothing and watch before sending them with the other pieces of physical evidence to the Analytical Laboratory in Lidcombe, in Sydney's western suburbs, for a more detailed study and analysis.

Once Judith's face had been cleaned, everyone present realised that the extent of her injuries was greater than first thought. Tim Lyons noted there was substantial bruising to the entire forehead and nose. Her nose was fractured and had a one-centimetre laceration. There were bruises and abrasions to both cheeks and an extensive bruise to Judith's lower lip.

Closer examination of the head revealed an 11-centimetre laceration on the right side of the forehead that ran across the eyebrow and curved back to the hairline. The underlying skull was fractured and depressed. Tim Lyons found some small, very fine shards of glass on the lower edge of the wound and two flakes deep inside the laceration. So deep were the flakes that Tim needed someone to hold the flesh aside with a surgical instrument while he manoeuvred them out. For the flakes to have been embedded so deeply demonstrated the force with which the object had struck Judith's forehead. The flakes were not glass, but an unknown substance. It was thought at the time they could be flecks of paint, but they would need to be forensically examined to determine their chemical makeup. Pieces of grit, resembling minute concrete, were also extracted from the wound.

Their thoughts went to the crime scene, where Peter Muscio had discovered a similar grit-like substance. There was also discussion about the fact that Ross's three boys and his friends from Singleton, Murray and Sally, had mentioned in passing about a figurine the family used as a doorstop. From all accounts it was a heavy statue, made of solid plaster or concrete, which would explain the grit found at the house. With the grit recovered from Judith's wounds, it would appear the statue was a likely weapon. The broken piece of ceramic in the main bedroom most probably also came from the statue, and the two flakes Tim recovered appeared to be consistent with paint from the figurine. Police were sure the statue had been painted, but more investigation would be needed to narrow the statue as being the murder weapon beyond doubt.

Continuing with the examination, Tim found another two-centimetre laceration above the right eyebrow. A ten-centimetre laceration was observed on the left side of the skull, about five centimetres above the left ear. The skin had been torn, but there was no skeletal damage under this wound. Two small glass fragments were retrieved from the edge of the laceration. Another four-centimetre laceration appeared on the vertex of the head.

Examining Judith's arms, Tim Lyons observed small cuts on her right forearm, as well as small shards of glass. Peter Fox immediately asked Tim if he thought the injuries, coupled with the glass fragments, were a result of Judith defending herself against an attack from a beer bottle. Tim admitted if Peter's theory were correct, he would have expected the forearm to display some bruising, but there was none. In Tim's opinion, however, that didn't mean Peter's theory wouldn't hold up. He certainly couldn't refute the idea. It was probable.

With respect to the glass fragments found on the body, Tim couldn't say with any accuracy whether the fragments were a result of the bottles being broken before death, at the time of death, or after death. The shards were very fine and Tim had to work very carefully to extract them without causing himself injury, similar to a needle stick injury.

Further examination revealed substantive bruising to both hands and the lower arms, as well as small scratches. A fracture had been sustained by the right hand. Tim believed all the cuts, abrasions, and bruising borne by the hands were consistent with defensive injuries against a heavy, solid object.

After the post mortem, Tim concluded that Judith Brown had died as a result of massive head injuries. The presence of significant abrasions to and lacerations of the head area with massive underlying skull fractures was consistent with the application of blunt force trauma of considerable magnitude. There was also evidence that while death did not occur immediately, it most likely occurred within a few minutes of the injuries being sustained.

As to the circumstances leading to Judith's murder, Tim couldn't be as conclusive as he was about her cause of death. He believed, as he did when he visited the crime scene, that Judith had been knocked to the floor, and that the greater extent of her injuries suggested her head might have been crushed against the floor by a heavy object being thrust down on it with great force. The perpetrator repeatedly struck Judith's head as she lay on the tiles. It had been a merciless and cowardly assault.

~

While the autopsy was being conducted, detectives were back at Nelson Bay Police Station re-evaluating the statements from Ross, the neighbours, Tavern staff and patrons, and prioritising their importance. They were looking for consistencies and, more importantly, inconsistencies, anything to help narrow the timeframe or information that may help direct their enquiries. Police would also decide if they had sufficient information or whether they required more detail from certain witnesses. Likewise, police would draw a list up of potential witnesses, people they knew might be of help but had yet to be interviewed, such as Judith's co-worker who had called at her home on the morning of the murder.

Although police had all the security videotapes from both bottle shops, they hadn't had the time to go through them. They also hadn't been through the register sales for the Friday afternoon to look for a purchase of two bottles of Toohey's New. At this stage, worrying about where Ross had bought two bottles of beer wasn't a priority.

As part of any investigation police need to look through their database and extract names of offenders whose modus operandi is similar to the crime. In this case, police looked at offenders with a history of break, enter, and steal who were known to live in or around the Hunter region. Checks were made with the Department of Corrective Services for any recent prison releases, as well as with local stations for any reports of home thefts.

Among the many names they found, there was one of particular interest, an offender who had a penchant for breaking into people's homes while they slept. It seemed he enjoyed taking the risk. Most housebreakers usually wait for the house to be empty of occupants, such as during working hours or holiday periods. Even though this offender usually operated at nights, he was still listed as a suspect and police would now have to track him down.

There were roughly five to six persons of interest that Task Force Saltpond detectives needed to interview before ruling them out of the investigation. Most, they knew, would not have committed the murder, but for the sake of thoroughness those persons still needed to be investigated. The last thing Peter wanted was to be accused of overlooking a potential suspect, however unlikely it was the person could have carried out the crime.

Another standard line of enquiry in any homicide investigation is to look closer at the victim's financial situation, to see who will gain from their death and if this was a possible motive. After all, it wouldn't be the first time a person had been killed because of greed.

Saltpond detectives prepared a brief for a magistrate to authorise the warrant giving police access to Ross and Judith's financial records. Police knew that Ross and Judith had sold their property in Singleton and were looking to buy a home in or near Anna Bay. They also knew that the couple had $80 000 in a fixed term account with the ANZ Bank. The receipt for this deposit was found on the night of the murder among the personal papers located in the main bedroom.

The warrant would give police the authority to contact banks and investigate Ross and Judith's spending habits, transfer of monies, income, and savings details. How much money did the couple have? Had they borrowed money from an unscrupulous source? Were the accounts in joint names or were either Judith or Ross the main signatory? Did they have separate accounts?

Police were anxious to speak with Ross and Judith's families and their close friends, to get a better understanding of their relationship and know more about their time together in Singleton. As well, police needed to know if there was a relative or someone the Brown family had known in the mining town who might have had a reason to harm Judith. Detectives organised themselves to travel to Singleton and begin conducting their enquiries.

With respect to the three boys, Peter felt it better to give them time to settle, to try to adjust to life without their mother. As they were all at school on the Friday it was not thought they would have information regarding their mother's death. Police would still need to speak with them, but there was no hurry.

The next time Peter was to speak with Ross was at the walk-through, and there were a lot of questions Peter and his team had prepared for him. They were curious why Ross had chosen to take his dog for a walk along Birubi Beach in such inclement weather and what his response would be to the circular bloodstain discovered on the top of the partition. Also, could Ross help them identify what, if anything, had been taken from the house?

Chapter 5

NARROWING THE FIELD OF SUSPECTS

Four days after Judith's murder, on Tuesday 6 June 2000, Ross Brown accompanied detectives back to the house. Peter Muscio, who had removed sections of carpet and tiles, had laid out sheets of black plastic across the floor of the crime scene to prevent any further contamination as he and his team still had control of the scene and hadn't yet finished conducting their examinations. Apart from the missing floor coverings, the inside of the house remained as it had been on the night of Judith's murder.

Ross had agreed to take part in the walk-through when he spoke to Peter Fox on the Friday night. Just as the first interview had been, the walk-through would also be videotaped. When they first arrived Ross, Peter, and Graeme Parker went to the rear of the house and congregated under the pergola. Ross began explaining the family's morning routine in greater detail, giving times when everyone woke and their preparations for the day. He repeated that he had taken Riley to school at 8.00 a.m. and returned to the house by 8.15. This time, though, he told the police that his dog, Floyd, accompanied them on their trip and sat inside the cabin of his vehicle. He remembered it had been bitterly cold, raining and 'blowin' a gale', not dissimilar to how the neighbours had described the morning.

While at home he saw Joel and Gene off to school before leaving the house himself at about nine o'clock, or maybe even some time before. This time when he left, he took the canopy off his utility, placed the dog on the tray, and then drove to Birubi Beach.

Peter and Graeme walked Ross around to the front of the house. Standing in the driveway Peter asked Ross to take them through his movements when he returned home that afternoon. He also warned Ross that when he entered the house to be careful as the floor was uneven; he also asked Ross not to touch anything. Ross acknowledged Peter's request and began his re-enactment.

As Ross was pulling up in the driveway on the Friday afternoon, he told police, he had been surprised to see Judith's car. Once he'd got out of his vehicle, he let the dog down from the tray. Ross then demonstrated how he carried the two beer bottles, one in his left hand and one under his left arm, and had his keys ready to open the door with his right. Opening the door, the dog ran ahead of him and into the house. Then, when he saw Judith's body, the bottles had fallen from his hand and from under his arm. Peter and Graeme watched carefully as Ross demonstrated what he was telling them.

During the examination made by Peter Muscio and the team of the crime scene, they were surprised, after hearing Ross's version of events, not to find a paper bag among the debris. It is commonplace for bottle shops to provide purchases wrapped in paper or plastic bags. In fact, there's a licensing law that prohibits any alcoholic beverage from being taken by a customer from a bottle shop without it being concealed in this way. Graeme put the question of the missing bag to Ross, who shrugged it off and quipped that he was 'saving trees'. Apparently, he had refused a bag.

Ross knew he'd also lost his glasses and dropped his keys, but he couldn't remember how that happened. He did remember kneeling with his wife for a number of minutes, but everything after that he claimed was 'patchy'.

Ross couldn't be sure what had happened to the dog, though he did recall walking into the main bedroom and seeing 'shit everywhere', a reference to the clothing, papers, and jewellery spread around the room. Asked if anything was missing, Ross examined the jewellery on the dresser. It was still spilled out as it had been on the Friday. Looking through the pieces Ross thought there was possibly a chain missing.

While still inside the house the afternoon of the murder Ross was able to secure the dog in the garage, and then ran out into the street to get help. He remembered people trying to calm him, explaining to the detectives, 'I can get upset, I've … I've got a pretty good … I can keep myself pretty steady and if I snap I do tend to like to do things I want and I don't want no one to stop me.'

Peter broached the question about the circular bloodstain visible on the wooden shelf of the brick partition. Ross shrugged, not knowing what could have caused the stain. As much as Peter pushed for Ross to try to give them some explanation for the bloodstain, Ross kept to his story: he had dropped the bottles upon entering the house. He was positive he hadn't placed a bottle on the ledge. Even when Peter offered possible alternatives, such as the stain coming from a vase, a drinking glass, a coffee mug, or some other circular object being on the surface at the time when Judith was killed, Ross refused to accept that anything had been placed there. 'No, mate ... never put anythin' up there ... As soon as you open the door, the wind'd blow the fuckin' thing off,' was his response.

In the laundry Ross indicated the basket of wet washing, telling police that he believed Judith had removed the clothes from the washing machine that morning. He also saw the nightie his wife had worn on the night before the murder, which was in a second clothesbasket with one of his flannel shirts that was grey in colour and bore the insignia of the open cut mine where he had worked. Even though both items were damp, Ross stated that the shirt would not have been washed at the same time as the other clothes. Other than conceding both items of clothing had been washed at some time, Ross offered no other reason for why they were damp.

Moving through the main area of the house, Ross mentioned that he couldn't see Judith's handbag. It should have been on the dining table together with her lunch and craft items for the daycare centre. The bag would have contained her purse, keys and other personal belongings. Ross was also sure a pair of football boots belonging to one of his sons was missing as well.

Standing at the spot where Judith's body had lain, Peter asked Ross if there was anything else missing. Ross looked around. He believed nothing else had been taken. Pointedly, Peter asked again, indicating with his hand towards the front door. 'What about in that area … Anything missing from there?'

Ross took a moment, and then realised something was missing. Rhetorically, he asked where the doorstop was. It was a ceramic statue that had stood by the door. The statue was of a swagman sitting on a log with his dog by his side. Ross's mother, who had three statues made, had given one to Ross and Judith as a gift, and another two to other members of the family. The statue, which the Browns had had in their possession for a number of years, was solid, not hollow, and quite heavy to lift; it had been painted in several colours. It was part of the family, fulfilling its service in Anna Bay as it had done in Singleton.

Hearing this, Peter and Graeme immediately knew they had formally identified their possible murder weapon. Due to Peter Muscio's earlier work in finding the piece of ceramic and the broken grit around the house, and putting them together with the grit and two flakes taken from Judith's body, police already suspected the statue was the weapon. They needed Ross to confirm that he hadn't removed the statue for any reason, and that the statue had been in the house on the morning of the murder. Further analysis would be needed to determine if the flakes taken from one of the wounds, believed to be paint, could be matched to the statue. Peter and Graeme now had a proper description of what they were looking for, though they'd still need to conduct examinations to be sure the Browns' statue was the weapon.

When talking about the statue, Ross squatted where Judith's body had lain, staring at the floor and wall. There were still minute fragments of ceramic on the floor and blood smears on the wall. Ross turned to Peter and asked if he could 'touch it', referring to one of the smears. Peter, somewhat taken aback by the request, wasn't sure how to respond. He paused a second, then gave Ross permission. Ross ran his finger through the smear, looked at his stained fingertip, wiped it clean, and said to himself, 'Oh, that's nothing'.

Should Judith have fallen victim to someone breaking into the house, and given that no signs of forced entry could be found, police were curious if any doors had been left unlocked. Police knew from Tina's statement that the rear sliding door had been left unlocked, though this could have also happened when the offender left. Standing in the garage, Ross assured police that the sliding door connecting the garage to the main area had been locked that morning. He couldn't speak for the rear sliding door.

Looking around the garage, Peter and Graeme noticed a bong, a device usually used for smoking illegal drugs, and a tin container with a small amount of cannabis, also called 'marijuana', inside. Cannabis is a prohibited drug. Ross admitted both items were his and that he did smoke the drug, though Judith disapproved of his habit. The two detectives confiscated the container and the bong. They had the right to charge Ross with possession of an illegal substance, but given the circumstances, Peter and Graeme felt it better to just take the items.

Satisfied that they had enough information from Ross on his movements within the house, Peter had organised for a four-wheel-drive vehicle to take himself, Graeme and Ross to Birubi Beach, and set off. They were curious why Ross would want to take Floyd to the sand dunes for between one and one and a half hours when the weather, even by his description, was cold and blustery. Peter couldn't imagine anyone wanting to be out in that weather when they could be inside in the warm.

Both detectives recalled how cold it had been that day, especially Graeme, whose long overcoat flapped in the wind as he stood outside the house. Ross, rejecting their sceptical tone, was adamant he'd done just that, taken his dog for its regular run on the beach. He just wanted to give his dog some exercise. He often did and the weather didn't put him off.

Reaching the beach, Ross showed detectives the track he drove down and where he stopped, letting his dog off the tray of his utility for its run. While they were there, Ross noticed some Asian tourists picking up pipis, small clam-like shellfish, from the shoreline. He shouted at the tourists, warning them that the 'cops are here', then turned to Peter and Graeme and told them they should go over and lock up the tourists. Ross laughed, but the detectives thought it odd behaviour, given the reason they were at the beach. Peter and Graeme thought Ross was treating the day as an excursion, ignoring its importance and relevance.

Arriving at the Anna Bay Tavern, Ross pointed out the exact spot he parked. When asked where he had purchased the two bottles of Toohey's New, Ross quickly pointed to the Tavern and said, 'That bottle shop there'.

Peter Fox wanted Ross to be sure and asked, 'That bottle shop here, attached to the pub [Tavern]?'

Ross gave an unequivocal, 'Yeah'.

Peter wondered how Ross, having spent most of the day drinking, could have afforded to stay at the Anna Bay Tavern all that time. Ross explained he had about $30 to $40 cash on him that day when he left the house. He agreed with Peter that it wasn't a lot of money. He admitted to the two detectives that he had borrowed a further $20 from a patron he knew at the Tavern in the afternoon, and had only $8 in his wallet when he returned home.

Having spent most the day with Ross retracing his movements, the detectives took him back to Clonmeen Circuit. Back at the house, Ross suddenly remembered something else. He told the detectives that he stopped at a service station on his way to Birubi Beach that

Friday morning. He purchased $10 or $15 worth of diesel. He even commented that he had struck a bird on the bonnet of his Toyota as he drove to the beach. The point about the service station had been left out when he made his original statement to police, for which Ross apologised as he had only just remembered.

Peter and Graeme noted this new piece of information. In their experience it isn't unusual for witnesses to remember finer points after an interview. They didn't treat Ross's omission of the service station as anything other than forgetfulness.

After the walk-through Peter and Graeme were still unsure if Ross had anything to do with Judith's murder. Most of what he had to say checked out, and what suspicions they had could be explained away. It was a difficult call to make during this early stage of the investigation.

There were a few things, mainly Ross's behaviour, that raised Peter and Graeme's concern during the walk-through. First, Ross had become a completely different person to the one they interviewed on the Friday evening. At that time Ross had been an angry man indulging in self-pity. Yet, come the Tuesday, the change in Ross's behaviour seemed remarkable. He addressed both detectives by their first names, as well as frequently referring to them as 'mate'. He was friendly and easy-going. At times, he'd even tried to engage the detectives by making jokes, as they'd witnessed at Birubi Beach. This suited Peter to a point, as he wanted Ross to be comfortable and speak freely, but Ross seemed to be totally disconnected from the events of the previous Friday.

Ross was very composed, extremely cooperative, and, surprisingly, quite matter of fact in recalling his movements on the day of Judith's murder. Peter had dealt with a number of people in similar circumstances to Ross, and he couldn't help but notice Ross's demeanour: it was very different to what he was used to and what he had expected.

'Here was a bloke walking around the house where his wife had died ... There was no emotion ... he was distant ... emotionally detached,' was how Peter Fox remembered Ross's behaviour.

'Ross acted as though nothing had happened ... like he was just showing us around a normal house, not the scene of Judy's murder.'

Ross's identification of the statue roused some suspicion. Peter and Graeme had already surmised, for reasons explained, that they were looking at the statue as the possible murder weapon. They also knew it had been in the house, as mentioned by Ross's sons and friends. Ross had to be asked twice, while standing at the spot where Judith's body had lain, if he remembered anything missing. Ross's hesitancy did give cause for suspicion, and again, Peter observed Ross's controlled emotions.

'The most remarkable part here was this man whose wife had just been murdered in that very same area and, literally, standing on the spot where Judith's body had been laying ... and [he] was totally unmoved by it ...

very clinical, very cold and very detached.'

When Ross asked to touch the blood smear, the way he looked at it, then discarded it, and the comment that it was 'nothing' also struck the detectives as being extremely odd behaviour. Peter and Graeme stared at each other. Neither could believe Ross's reactions—or lack of—to the scene. They found his behaviour remarkable, especially after his emotional outbursts on the Friday. Still, Ross's behaviour wasn't enough to prove guilt and didn't further the investigation, but it did leave an impression on Peter and Graeme.

News of the walk-through reached some of the media. Naturally, they were curious and felt that Ross might be considered a suspect. Peter Fox quickly corrected the speculation, responding to media enquiries with, 'He [Ross] is one of a number of people who we have been spoken to'.

Immediate calls were made in an attempt to locate a replica of the swagman statue. It was an unusual statue, in that none of the retail outlets stocking figurines had anything similar. Finally, police spoke to Ross's stepmother who put them in touch with Ross's aunt in Singleton, who still had her figurine, so police borrowed it for a press conference.

Police sent out details to all media outlets, informing them of the statue and Judith's missing handbag. They described the bag as being leather, brown in colour, with a gold clasp, and containing a wallet, keys, money, and credit cards in her name.

Before parading the suspected murder weapon before the media, Peter Fox took it to Tim Lyons. The statue, which stood 30 centimetres tall, was made of solid concrete. It weighed around eight kilograms, something that could not be easily lifted with one hand. Given the intensity of Judith's fractures, together with the grit and flakes of paint found at the scene and on Judith's body, Tim Lyons concluded that the statue was most likely the murder weapon. Judith's injuries were certainly consistent with being made by something with the weight and composed of the same material as the aunt's statue. Peter made the decision: he definitely had his murder weapon.

A press conference was called for Thursday 8 June. Peter addressed the gathering and displayed the swagman statue the taskforce had collected from Ross's aunt. He explained that the statue was believed to be the murder weapon; family members had stated they last saw it on the Friday morning. 'The family remembers seeing it at the door, but when we conducted crime scene evidence it was gone.

'Extensive searches around the house were conducted, but it could have been dumped anywhere ... Anna Bay has beaches and sand dunes ... There is more chance of the public coming across it than police.'

While the display statue was painted, it had been painted in different colours to the one Judith and Ross owned. In fact Ross's mother had all three statues individually painted to reflect the colour of each family's dog. Their swagman was grey, and sat on a brown log with a black dog by his side. The aunt's swaggie had a blue shirt, grey vest, dark blue trousers, and sat on a black log; the dog had been painted rust brown.

When asked if robbery was a motive, especially as Judith's handbag was also missing, Peter responded, 'We believe we will get close to establishing a motive if we find the statue'.

One question police still had was: Why would the killer take the statue? After all, it was an item unique to that household. While it had been used as a murder weapon, would it matter if the attacker had left the statue? It didn't make a lot of sense, unless the statue held evidence, such as fingerprints or blood, that linked it to the offender. Whatever the reason, the killer obviously felt it was important to cart it away and have it disposed of.

Though no one had found Judith's handbag or its contents, the response to the statue when its existence had been publicised was overwhelming. It became apparent to police that people understood they were looking for a ceramic or cement figurine, but it became clear that the exact item had been lost in translation. Even with a detailed description and the image of the aunt's statue being flashed across television screens, any unsuspecting household figurines, particularly garden gnomes without a home, were seized and turned in to police.

Peter Fox accumulated up to thirty very different styles of gnomes and other statues in varying states of disrepair; none of them being the Browns' swagman or anything that resembled it. They had been brought in from waste facilities, abandoned properties, and building sites. As the collection began to grow and Peter's office became overcrowded with the small fellows, a colleague stood at the door one day and said, 'Foxy, you fit right in there … You're definitely the king of the garden gnomes.'

Eventually, a couple from the town of Rutherford, 60 kilometres west of Anna Bay, found a suspicious-looking statue and turned it in to police. It was a statue of a swagman with his head broken off; he was sitting on a log with his dog next to him. Unfortunately, it wasn't the murder weapon. This statue was unpainted and didn't have a section missing from the back. It was, however, an identical copy, which Peter and his team were happy to keep. After Peter glued the head back on, it became useful as the investigation progressed.

⁓

Peter Muscio had completed his examinations of the Clonmeen Circuit house by Wednesday 7 June. Ross, with the help of friends from Singleton, had removed all his belongings soon after. The keys of the house were then returned to the real estate agent, who decided to replace all the carpet and try to attract new tenants.

With the house still vacant and before the new carpet was put in, Peter Fox arranged with the agents to conduct a test. Peter was still curious about the dropping of the beer bottles. On the night of the murder he remembered finding shards of glass metres away from where the bottles had been dropped. Peter wanted to know if the glass would travel so far after only being dropped, or whether more force had to be used for the glass to fly a great distance.

Peter Muscio agreed to help. He completely covered his body to protect himself from the glass. With a dozen bottles of beer to go through, Peter Muscio re-enacted Ross's movements and dropped two bottles on the tiled floor. He repeated this six times. After every test the area was cleaned before the following test took place.

As much as they tried to get some reliable measure of how far the glass would travel when the bottles were dropped, the results each time were so random that they were inconclusive. There was no way of knowing if Ross dropped the bottles as he said, or if they had been thrown down.

Speaking with relatives and friends, police were able to put together a good overview of Ross and Judith's lives, from early childhood through to their married life together. Police already knew from Ross that he was an only child and that his mother had died when he was an infant. Ross's father was not a miner, as he had told the nurses at the clinic the night of the murder, but a publican, who managed a hotel in Singleton. His father remarried Paula, who was working at the hotel, and together they raised Ross.

The Browns moved around a bit, still managing hotels in and around the Hunter district, before settling down in Wallsend, an outer western suburb of Newcastle. Paula described her son as a good child and natural athlete in his early years. During his teens, however, he became a troublesome youth, mixed with bad company, experimented with drugs, and reportedly told lies and stole. Despite Ross's rebellious nature, and because he was her only child, Paula felt they had a strong bond.

Judith had been the second child in a family of five children. She did well at school and was the school captain of her primary school. Having sat for her School Certificate in Year 10, Judith made the decision not to go on to Year 11 and secured employment with the Steggles Chicken processing plant at Beresfield, a small regional town between Newcastle and Maitland. It was while working at Steggles in the late 1970s that she met Ross. This was at the time when Judith's family lived at Barnsley, just a few minutes southwest of where Ross was living in Wallsend.

After beginning their relationship Judith and Ross travelled to Queensland, where they lived and worked in various towns up and down the coast. As much as Judith seemed to be an opposite of Ross, Judith's family weren't too surprised by the attraction. From what family members told police, Judith had always been attracted to the 'bad boys'. She seemed to like the tattoos, motorcycles, and apparently rebellious behaviour.

In the early 1980s Judith's parents decided on a sea change and moved to Queensland. During this time,

Judith and Ross had a falling out and Judith stayed with her parents. After a few weeks the couple reconciled and Judith and Ross were married in Gladstone, just south of Rockhampton, on Queensland's central coast in 1983.

Not long after the wedding Judith fell pregnant. Ross and Judith then travelled back to Newcastle to visit family and friends. Police were told that Ross returned to his family home at Wallsend, and requested a large sum of money to settle his debts. As Ross and his parents entered into a discussion about the money, Judith allegedly became upset and told her in-laws that Ross owed the money for drugs. Whether Ross received the money or not is unclear, but Ross and Judith did travel back to Queensland where their first son, Riley, was born at Bundaberg on the coral coast in October 1984. The young family remained in Queensland, moving about wherever the work was, before relocating to Coffs Harbour, on the central coast of New South Wales.

In the late 1980s Ross and Judith moved to Singleton in the Upper Hunter. With the help of family members, Ross secured a position at Howick open cut mine. Judith found work as a waitress in a local club. They decided to settle and give their transient lifestyle away. Their second son, Joel, was born in September 1988.

After Joel's birth, Judith and Ross bought their first home. Judith decided to become a nurse and completed a course at Newcastle Hospital. She then took up a position as an assistant nurse at Elizabeth Gates Nursing Home in Singleton.

Family and friends agreed that on the whole Ross and Judith seemed happy together and as a family. It appeared that domestic life was going well. Some did make the comment to police that the family's stability was due to a large extent to Judith, who had control of the finances. Apparently, from what police were told, Ross was something of a spendthrift and didn't manage money well.

In late 1991 Ross's father died and he didn't leave a will. A dispute broke out between Ross and Paula over the ownership of the family home. Ross's father had brought a property at Tanilba Bay on the Tilligerry Peninsula in the waters of Port Stephens. The township is over 42 kilometres north of Newcastle and just 10 kilometres as the crow flies from Anna Bay. To resolve the matter between mother and son, Paula agreed to sell the house, pay off all debts still owing on the estate and to split the remaining money equally with Ross.

It was alleged that as the sale was being processed, Ross went back on his deal and refused to sell. An argument erupted again and in frustration Paula walked away, giving the house to Ross. It was this matter that created the estrangement between them. They did not speak to each other again until the night of Judith's murder.

Judith distanced herself from the dispute between Ross and his stepmother. She didn't want anything to do with it and left it for Ross to sort out. From all reports there were few disputes between Judith and Ross.

As stated, Judith managed the finances. Police would also discover that Judith handed out a weekly allowance to Ross, his pocket money, which he could spend as he wished. He also rented out the Tanilba Bay house, which earned him a fortnightly income of around $350. According to people police spoke to, Ross was very possessive of the property and insisted it was his, that Judith had nothing to do with it, that she had no claim on any of the rent money.

Through the 1990s Ross and Judith settled into a domesticated life, building a network of friends and becoming involved with their boys' sporting activities. Their youngest son was born in March 1993. To show their love of rugby league, he was given Gene as his first name and the middle name of Lewis, after two of Queensland's greatest State of Origin Rugby League stars, Gene Miles and Wally Lewis.

All three boys seemed to take after their father in being natural athletes, and took up playing junior rugby league. Judith and Ross were great supporters and were known never to miss a game. Riley's team won its grand final in 1999, the year before the family moved to Anna Bay.

Still in Singleton, Ross continued working at the open cut mine until 1998, when Howick's offered workers voluntary redundancies. Ross and Judith decided to accept the employer's offer. They sold their Singleton home in January 1999, and Ross's redundancy package came through in September the same year. After all their debts were paid off, the couple had $27 000 remaining. Judith put $15 000 of that money into a fixed term deposit.

Despite enquiries, police were unable to establish exactly why Ross accepted the redundancy because his job at the mine was paying him over $100 000 a year. Police couldn't understand why he would want to leave secure employment, particularly as he had a young family.

Voluntary redundancies are usually offered when an employer wants to restructure his workforce. In most cases those employees who accept the offer are not replaced, but that doesn't mean that those who don't take the redundancy and decide to remain with the company are at risk of losing their positions.

Ross seemed too young to be taking a voluntary redundancy. He was only 44 at the time and had plenty of work years ahead of him. According to Ross, he and Judith just wanted a change. It wasn't that police necessarily believed there was anything suspicious in the decision, but they just needed to know the details.

In January 2000, the Browns made the move to their rental accommodation at 24 Clonmeen Circuit, Anna Bay, at the same time looking for a home to purchase. Judith found employment with a local retirement village, while Ross took a job driving a bobcat, a mini dozer, for a company in Newcastle. Not long after, Ross had a falling out with his employer and picked up another job with Booral, working in their gravel quarry.

Judith also changed her employment, going from the retirement village to being a care worker at the Salamander Childcare Centre.

Police were told that while Ross and Judith appeared happy with their move, Judith was concerned about their finances because they had been using their savings. She was, however, optimistic and keen to buy a house. They had inspected a property, but attempts to borrow the funds failed as Ross didn't have permanent employment.

Police would later discover that Ross had withdrawn in excess of $12 000, completely exhausting the balance of one of their accounts. In his interview with Peter and Graeme on the Friday night, Ross did speak about having spent a lot of money on new furnishings and other items for the house and the Browns' Clonmeen Circuit home did appear to have new furniture and appliances.

During the six months the Browns were in Anna Bay, Ross became the domestic housekeeper, walked the dog, drove his boys to school and sporting commitments, and in the latter weeks began spending most of his afternoons at the Anna Bay Tavern. From what police had discovered as they spoke to relatives and friends, Judith had not been happy with Ross spending so much time drinking.

Immediately following the day of the murder, Ross took his family to stay with Judith's brother before returning to Singleton, where he stayed with Murray and Sally. On Sunday 4 June, two days after Judith's death, Ross went with Riley to see him play rugby league in Newcastle. While at the game, Ross spoke with friends and borrowed some money from them.

Because of their sons' sporting prowess, Ross and Judith were well known by members of their local rugby league club. On that Sunday, to show respect for the family's loss, the first grade team wore black armbands onto the field.

All of the family and friends police had spoken to recalled that Ross told them the same sequence of events for the Friday as he had told the police. He apparently didn't go into great detail, but from what was relayed back to police, Ross's story had remained consistent.

It would take investigators on Task Force Saltpond two weeks to track down all their persons of interest and then to check their stories before deciding what, if any, further enquiries should be conducted. Each of the potential suspects had, to use a cliché, rock-solid alibis. They either had witnesses, or were nowhere near Clonmeen Circuit, let alone Anna Bay, on the Friday.

Even the offender who police thought may have been a good candidate for the murder was quickly ruled out. Peter Fox had tracked him down at his place of employment, a construction site. After speaking with the former thief, Peter verified his story with his building supervisor. The supervisor was succinct in his answer: 'I had him up on that roof the whole day … and I don't know him well enough to lie for him.'

Investigators like to work quickly to determine who is a suspect and who isn't, so as to narrow their enquiries down to a few potential suspects. Finding out what the suspect's alibi is and checking on it helps save resources being wasted on dead ends, and so enables more time to be spent on collecting evidence. For Peter Fox and his team, their list of suspects had dwindled to where they were left with none. There was now no one who had previously been caught by police, or who had been mentioned to them as a possible suspect, who could have committed the murder. Eliminating their list of suspects left Peter with only one name—Ross Ernest Brown.

Even with Ross as the only possible suspect, there hadn't been enough evidence presented to indicate whether he was Judith's murderer. While the field of suspects had been narrowed, Peter and his team had to keep an open mind. There could still be someone else out there who had killed Judith.

Numerous calls had been made to Crime Stoppers and Nelson Bay Police Station in response to all the media surrounding the case. Every call was followed up, however insignificant it might have appeared. Whether police had the contact details of the caller or if the information was left anonymously, investigators made enquiries to determine its value. This included calls from clairvoyants.

In Peter Fox's experience it isn't unusual for clairvoyants to make contact with an investigation to offer their unique insight. Peter, though, has yet to hear from a clairvoyant who can offer any useful information. None of the exponents of the paranormal had ever been correct with what they've had to say to him about a case.

Even so, Peter does keep an open mind. As with any other call received by police, the investigators on Task Force Saltpond followed up information supplied by clairvoyants. One psychic suggested that the statue police were looking for had been dumped on a beach in Queensland. While it seemed unlikely, Peter contacted Queensland Police, who organised for the beach to be searched. They found nothing.

One of the reasons why every little snippet of information is considered important is because there's no knowing if the killer or an associate has called to reveal some evidence. Some criminals like to taunt the police, to attempt to mislead the investigation or offer sketchy but accurate details, while others will give up everything, perhaps hoping they'll be caught. Police cannot afford to ignore or quickly dismiss any lead that comes to them, especially in a homicide investigation where evidence is sparse and suspects are few.

On Thursday 15 June, detectives from Task Force Saltpond went to Singleton and spoke with Judith and Ross's three boys. Peter Fox's delay in speaking with them was deliberate. He wanted to give the boys some grieving time and for them to try to settle after the trauma of losing their mother. Gene, the youngest son, didn't have much of a memory of the Friday, while Joel gave a good account of events for the morning.

Joel stated that Ross had taken Floyd, their Staffordshire terrier, with him when he drove Riley to school. Ross apparently did this because he intended to go straight on to the beach to exercise the dog. However, Ross returned home with Floyd before the other two boys had left for school. The children kissed both parents goodbye and began their walk to school at 8.40. Joel told detectives that he recalled his father was wearing a grey flannel shirt and black tracksuit pants that morning, not the clothing he wore in the afternoon. Joel added that he had seen his father drive past him in the direction of home about fifteen minutes later, when he was standing in the school yard.

On the Friday afternoon, Joel had rugby league practice at Valentine, just south of Newcastle. He had been expecting his father to drive him and another boy who lived around the corner to practice. It was a regular Friday afternoon routine.

Riley confirmed his father had driven him to school in the morning, and that Floyd had been in the vehicle. He informed the detectives that Ross would normally pick him up in the afternoon, but couldn't say why his father had neglected to do so on the Friday of the murder. The only reasons why his father would not have collected him from school would be if Ross had a job interview or had to visit Centrelink for some reason. Riley also confirmed that Ross was expected to take Joel and another boy to league training at Valentine in the afternoon once his younger brother had arrived home from school.

Two weeks to the day after she had been slain in her own home, on Friday 16 June 2000, family and friends gave Judith Brown a solemn farewell. The funeral was held at the All Saints Anglican Church in Singleton, and then her body was taken for burial at the Anglican Lawn Cemetery. Around 500 people attended the service, demonstrating how popular and much-loved Judith was in her adopted home town. Detectives from Task Force Saltpond joined relatives and friends at the service to show their support for Judith's family, for Ross, and their three boys.

Following the service, Ross was observed slapping the backs of people and telling jokes. Again, his behaviour raised the eyebrows of taskforce detectives. Ross also managed to visibly upset members of Judith's family and some close friends, who felt his actions were inappropriate.

Chapter 6

LIES, SUSPICIONS AND DOGGEDNESS

In the weeks following Judith's murder, police were still left with more questions than answers. They were still awaiting the results from the physical evidence collected at the scene, and what leads they did have had not advanced the investigation. Police were, however, sure of two important points.

First, the statuette used by the Browns was the murder weapon. As well as the tests conducted by Tim Lyons, and the physical evidence recovered from the scene by Peter Muscio, Task Force Saltpond investigators were able to track down the maker of the figurine. He lived and worked out of a workshop in Tanilba Bay, a small coastal town where Paula had purchased the statues while she and Ross's father lived there.

The craftsman explained that he hand-painted the statuettes to order. Police obtained a copy of the swagman from Ross's aunt and sent it to the Analytical Laboratories in Lidcombe, where the paint on the statues was checked against the two flakes found in the head wound. The paint matched, showing it was the same chemical makeup as that on the other statues. This meant the flakes of paint came from a statue painted with the same type of paint used on the other, and was the final confirmation police needed to be sure the figurine was the murder weapon.

The time of death was the other fact that police held to be correct. Amazingly for Peter Fox and other sceptical police, it appeared Judith's watch had stopped at or very near the time of the attack. It had been verified by a watch expert that the impact, together with the viscosity of the blood, would certainly have caused the mechanism in the watch to cease working. The watch would have stopped immediately or within a few seconds of the attack.

Just how accurate was the timepiece? Peter and his team could only speculate, but given that Judith worked as a nurse's assistant it was agreed that she would have had to keep the watch set on the precise time. Peter could think of no reason why Judith would have deviated from this practice while working at the childcare centre. His intuition was proved right by those who had worked with Judith, who all commented on her punctuality. So, police had now established that Judith was killed at or very near 9.14.28 on Friday 2 June 2000.

The problem facing Task Force Saltpond investigators was their lack of suspects. One by one all potential suspects had been eliminated, and the investigation kept coming back to Ross. Even so, police weren't convinced Ross was a serious suspect in the murder of his wife. It didn't mean they weren't suspicious; it was more a case of not having anything that, from an evidentiary point of view, would warrant police taking a closer look.

They checked Ross's statement by speaking with the Anna Bay Tavern patrons and viewing security video footage, all of which seemed to corroborate his story. But the taskforce couldn't verify if he had purchased the two bottles of Toohey's New from either of the bottle shops. The cash register receipts didn't show a sale of just two beers and the security footage was jumpy and hard to make out. From all the cameras in the Tavern, the video had recorded vision that changed views every few seconds, from the bar area, to the front of the bottleshop, to the back of the store, and so on.

While Peter Fox still had use of the detectives working on the taskforce, he decided to review Ross's statement once more. He wanted to see all the security footage from the Anna Bay Tavern and the two bottle shops, and have all the witness statements gone over again. He arranged for the security tapes to be redubbed so that only one camera angle could be viewed on an individual tape. This meant detectives could watch the area of the bottle shop they wanted without it cutting away. Should they see Ross, they would then cue the other tapes using the time code to track his movements within the shop. They would easily see if he had purchased anything, then compare the time with the sales receipts, taking in the variance of the times that Peter Wright had discovered when he collected the tapes.

The purpose of this closer scrutiny was to attempt to

eliminate Ross from their enquiries once and for all so they could move on. If he was guilty, then something had to show up that would give police cause to concentrate their efforts.

There were already a couple of things that had raised Peter Fox's suspicions. The patrons at the Tavern had stated that Ross normally arrived at lunchtime and only stayed a couple of hours at the most. Yet, Ross admitted that, on that Friday, he was drinking from 10.30 a.m. until after 2.00 p.m., almost four hours. There was also Riley's statement, which claimed Ross usually picked him up after school and that he was supposed to have driven Riley and a friend to league practice that afternoon but didn't.

Being at the Tavern during those hours didn't necessarily mean Ross was guilty, but it did make Peter curious. Drinking at the Tavern for nearly four hours could be explained quite simply: Ross had just decided to spend more time there that particular day. It could simply be a coincidence. But why didn't he bother collecting Riley on his way home, particularly as he did this regularly?

Peter also sent detectives to speak with the staff at the service station where Ross said he purchased $10 or $15 worth of diesel. As with the bottle shops, Peter wanted the cash register receipts and any security footage showing customers' comings and goings.

It is a long and exhausting process, but every single second of all the security vision from the bottle shops had to be viewed and every customer logged as to when they entered the premises and what they purchased, which would then be checked against the sales receipts and when they left. While some of the footage was grainy and less than clear, Peter decided that customers would be identified by their clothing and gender. Knowing what Ross was wearing would make it easier for police to pick him out of a crowd of customers. It meant they weren't relying solely on facial features.

Sitting down to watch the footage from the Anna Bay Tavern, Peter noticed something a little disturbing about Ross. Other police had previously viewed the tape to check how long Ross remained at the premises, but Peter decided to watch more carefully; he began counting. From the start of the tape, which began after Ross's arrival, to when Ross and another patron left the bar area, Peter counted twelve schooners of beer, that is, in the four hours Ross spent at the Tavern, he consumed twelve times 425 millilitres of beer.

The alcohol consumption guidelines recommend two standard drinks in the first hour, then one standard drink every hour after that for men to remain under or on the .05 limit for driving. A standard drink is measured by one middy (285 millilitres) of full-strength beer, less than two-thirds per drink of the amount Ross was consuming. Seeing the number of beers Ross had knocked back, it now didn't surprise Peter that he had acted so irrationally on the Friday afternoon.

Again from what patrons and staff who knew Ross had told police, he normally only ever drank between two to four schooners, or even just had a lemon squash.

To be drinking so heavily seemed an odd change of behaviour. It had been established that Ross liked a beer; he also liked to gamble. Seeing Ross knock back so many beers certainly raised suspicion in Peter and the other detectives' minds. After all, how would Ross expect to drive his son to league practice in that state? It couldn't be coincidence. There had to be another reason.

Detectives looking through the security footage from the two bottle shops—the Anna Bay Tavern's and Abb's—couldn't find a record of Ross purchasing the beer. They viewed every single camera angle and the closest they came was seeing Ross enter, walk around and then walk out. What was interesting was that, according to the security video, Ross didn't go into the Anna Bay Tavern bottle shop at any time on the Friday. Despite what he had told police, there simply was no footage of him being in the shop. Where police did find Ross was at Abb's Bottle Shop, up the road from the Tavern, but he hadn't made a purchase. He didn't buy beer or anything else. He had simply walked into Abb's, wandered around, and then walked out empty-handed.

Cash register receipts from both bottle shops were thoroughly checked: neither showed a sale of two long-necked bottles of Toohey's New beer at any time throughout the day. When scrutinising the tapes and the receipts, police covered the whole day and looked for anyone or any sign of someone buying the two bottles of beer, just in case Ross had had someone buy them for him or if he'd somehow sneaked in without being caught on any of the cameras, as unlikely as that was.

For the first time, here was a proven contradiction in Ross's statement to police: there was no evidence of Ross having purchased the beers on the way home, or at any other time during the day. If he didn't buy the two bottles of beer, how were they broken when he walked into the house? And why was he so insistent that he had bought the two bottles at the Tavern's bottle shop on his way home?

According to Ross's version of events he didn't leave the Anna Bay Tavern alone. He was in the company of another patron whom he had offered to give a lift home. Peter read the statement the patron had given to his detectives. It confirmed Ross's version of events, that the two men left the Tavern at around 2.00 that afternoon and then returned soon after. It didn't mention anything about Ross going to the bottle shop to purchase his beers. The detectives who asked the patron questions had been focused on establishing the time Ross left the Tavern, not whether he visited the bottle shop.

Peter eventually tracked down and spoke to the patron who had left with Ross. The patron, Joe, had accepted Ross's offer of a lift, but as they began their journey Joe decided he wanted to buy some alcohol to take home. Ross pulled up at Abb's Bottle Shop, not the Tavern bottle shop. Peter wanted to be sure Joe's recollection was right and asked him how he could be so certain it was Abb's.

Joe and Ross were had set off from the Anna Bay Tavern in the Toyota HiLux four-wheel-drive when Joe decided he wanted to purchase a carton of beer. He also remembered Ross said to him, specifically, he needed to buy two bottles of Toohey's New. Ross parked his vehicle at Abb's Bottle Shop, as it was on the way. The two men went into the shop. After Joe had made his purchase he left the store and waited for Ross by the vehicle. Ross, empty-handed, soon followed.

Joe reiterated that he was sure Ross didn't have any bottles of beer because he asked him why he hadn't bought any. Ross told him that because he was 10 cents short the sales assistant wouldn't let him have the beers. Hearing this, Peter asked why Ross didn't just buy one. Joe couldn't give a reason. He did say that Ross appeared 'pissed off' as he and Ross drove away. Joe then saw a person he wanted to catch up with. Ross turned his four-wheel-drive around and drove back to the Tavern.

The thought that Ross would not be allowed to buy any beer because he was just 10 cents short didn't ring true for Peter. He went into Abb's Bottle Shop and spoke to the proprietor and the sales assistant who had been on duty on the Friday. The sales assistant knew Ross well and regarded him as a regular customer. He remembered Ross coming into the store on the afternoon, but couldn't recall if Ross had bought anything or whether he just walked in and walked out. Peter asked whether, if Ross had wanted to buy two bottles of Toohey's New and was 10 cents short, the sales assistant would refuse his purchase. In response, the sales assistant pulled open a drawer under the cash register that contained loose coins, mostly 20-, 10- and 5-cent pieces. He told Peter that customers are always walking out of the store, leaving their small change behind. The staff toss the change in the drawer and, if a local is a few cents short of the price, he and other staff members make up the difference from the loose change. They'll do this for any of their regulars. They do it so the cash register balances at the end of trade. And, yes, he would have made up the difference for Ross if he had been 10 cents short.

Peter had definitely caught Ross out in a lie. None of the evidence supported Ross's story of buying beer on his way home. But why lie about it? Peter had a theory. Thinking back to the crime scene, Peter remembered the circular bloodstain found on the top of the brick partition.

On the night it was found, police believed that the most likely source of the mark was the bottom of a beer bottle. Although the faint ridging around the stain matched the beer bottles, it wasn't conclusive; the stain might have been caused by another, as yet to be identified, object. Still, working on the premise that it was the beer bottle, Peter theorised that Ross had broken one bottle, while the second bottle, having come in contact with Judith's blood, was picked up and placed on the partition.

If this theory were correct, then Peter felt that the first beer bottle was broken at the time of Judith's murder. This meant that Ross, who had been so emphatic that he'd purchased the bottles on his way home and broken them that afternoon, had actually broken one during the morning when he killed his wife.

After leaving the house and drinking heavily he would have been thinking of ways to cover the broken bottle. Unlike the statue, which he was able to dispose of, he might have thought he couldn't clean up the broken glass, as it would be too difficult and too obvious, so he needed to devise a story to explain the breakage. He decided to tell police that he had broken the bottles when he arrived home. It would make sense and, he probably thought, how would police know when the bottles were broken?

Leaving the Tavern he had possibly still been thinking about the bottles, which could explain why he told his friend Joe that he needed two bottles of Toohey's New. But if he had purchased two bottles, how would he account for the broken one in the house? Most likely he would have had to break those two as well, or dispose of them before he arrived home. When Ross arrived home, Peter continued to theorise. He walked in, saw the bottle still on the partition, and, to confuse the scene and support his story he dropped the remaining bottle. This would explain why Tina and Judith's co-worker had not noticed any seepage coming from under the front door in the morning but why it had been noticeable in the afternoon. Ross might also have broken the second bottle for the benefit of anyone listening, to help fit his story.

Peter's scenario was given weight by the physical evidence at the scene, Ross's insistence that he brought the bottles in the afternoon and the fact that he hadn't. However, unless Ross admitted to this, there would be no way of knowing if Peter was correct. It was just a theory. Even so, having established that Ross lied to police about purchasing the beer increased his status as a suspect. In fact, Ross was their only suspect, which didn't mean Peter wasn't still keeping an open mind. His years as a detective had taught him never to put all his eggs in one basket. Police might receive information, through a tipoff or from the results of the physical evidence, that supported another scenario and puts a new suspect in their sights. It can happen, and it has.

The other question Peter had was: when did Ross buy $10 or $15 worth of diesel? Could the purchase of the fuel help Peter and his detectives establish a better timeframe of Ross's movements? Did he purchase it before or after nine o'clock?

Unfortunately, enquiries made at the service station proved fruitless. The attendant couldn't recall Ross as a customer on the Friday. There were no sales registered to show the purchase of $10 or $15 worth of diesel. The cash register didn't record sales unless a customer asked for a receipt and the console operator obliged. So, if Ross paid cash, the money would have been put straight into the till. In case Ross had not paid by cash, police went through the credit card receipts, but they didn't find any sales of diesel. To add to their woes, the service station didn't employ surveillance cameras, so there was no vision available of that Friday's customers.

While the service station drew a blank, the fact that Ross mentioned the purchase of diesel did prove to be of interest to the detectives. Ross, by his own admission, only had $30 to $40 in his pocket on the Friday morning. Then, after he had bought the diesel he would have realised he didn't have enough cash to spend at the Anna Bay Tavern. Had he returned home to possibly borrow some from Judith? Did Ross then get into an argument with Judith over money, or over spending the day at the pub, and did the argument get out of control and result in Ross striking out and murdering his wife?

It was still only guesswork. No neighbour had come forward to say they had heard Ross and Judith arguing that morning, or on any other day for that matter. Based on all the information it had gathered, Task Force Saltpond was long on theories but short on evidence.

There was one witness statement that seemed to have been overlooked until now. It was the statement made by a neighbour living adjacent to Ross and Judith's house. The neighbour was Danni (not her real name), who knew Ross and Judith well enough to wave hello each day. On the Friday she stated that, as she left for work, she couldn't see Judith's green Daewoo because Ross's HiLux was blocking her view; the view from her home looks across to the Browns', with the driveway in the foreground. Danni said she left for work at about ten past nine.

If Danni was right about the time, then Peter might just be narrowing the time Ross claimed he left

Clonmeen Circuit.

Standing at Danni's front door, Peter looked across the street. To his right he could see Ross and Judith's house, with their driveway clearly in the foreground. If Ross's Toyota HiLux had been parked on the left of their driveway, it would certainly have blocked any view of Judith's small, green Daewoo.

Speaking with Danni, Peter stressed how important it was for Danni to be sure of the time. Danni explained she would take her children to school, then return home and get ready for work. She remembered checking her clock before she left. It said ten past nine. She always left for work each day between ten and twenty past. As she exited her front door she looked towards the Browns', but couldn't recall, when asked by an earlier policeman, seeing Judith's car because Ross's vehicle had blocked her view. But she was sure of the time and what she had seen.

Peter found Danni to be a credible witness. While her statement put Ross at the house after nine, it still wasn't enough. Any defence counsel could argue whether Danni had actually looked at her clock, and whether it was accurate. Unfortunately, there was nothing else to support her recollection of time. She didn't see anyone else, she wasn't talking to anyone on the phone, and there was nothing to substantiate the time. Basically, it was only her word that she had seen Ross's four-wheel-drive at ten past nine that Friday morning.

As the weeks went on, the number of detectives working on Task Force Saltpond dwindled from around a dozen on the first weekend, to eight, then to two, and eventually to one: Peter Fox. He was left to continue to follow up on leads and try to unravel the how, why, and who murdered Judith Brown.

The reduction in resources within the taskforce wasn't a reflection of the lack of evidence or belief the case would not be solved, but rather as part of a natural attrition that saw local detectives being put on other cases or resuming the cases they had been pulled away from. The criminal world doesn't stop to wait for police to finish one inquiry before committing an offence and giving them their next job. Life goes on. Even Peter, as determined as he was to solve Judith's murder, was also assigned other duties.

~

Peter Fox is the eldest in a family of four. He was brought up in Green Valley in Sydney's west during the 1960s and 1970s. Green Valley was a new suburb when Peter's family settled there; later it became a tough, working-class Housing Commission estate area. His father was a World War II veteran, his mother a country girl. Peter's father earned what he could, going from job to job, making sure his young family had the essentials— food, shelter and clothing. Life was obviously hard, and Peter remembered the neighbourhood as being violent and, at times, out of control.

One afternoon as the teenaged Peter was making his way home from school, he was set upon and bashed.

One of his front teeth was kicked out during the assault. When Peter arrived home, shaken and bloodied, the police were called. This was Peter's first contact with detectives. They took his statement and eventually charged the offenders. It was an unpleasant period in his life.

It wasn't that his assailants had been caught that had made an impression on the young Peter, but the compassion and professionalism of the detectives who had dealt with his case. He decided then that he wanted to have a career in policing, wanted to be in a position where he could help people as he had been helped. It was definitely the job for him.

Peter hoped to leave school early and join the police cadets. The police cadet program doesn't exist any more, but at the time the New South Wales Police Force recruitment section usually favoured taking in men and women who had spent time as cadets. In fact, it was a natural progression for cadets to go straight into the academy. Unfortunately, Peter wasn't successful in getting into the cadets and continued his schooling to get his Higher School Certificate, hoping this would give him an advantage.

The first two times Peter applied for the police he was unsuccessful. He had a fallback plan, though, and that was to join the army if the police wouldn't take him. Not one to give up easily, Peter applied to the police a third and final time. The recruitment section gave applicants only three attempts. This time he succeeded. He began his eleven-week training with 164 other recruits at the Police Barracks in Redfern in April 1978. These days police have thirteen-week training, but must also complete an undergraduate university degree in policing prior to being accepted.

Having completed their training the 165 graduates, unkindly referred to by experienced police as 'eleven-week wonders', were dispatched to police stations across the state. Peter and twelve other probationary constables were stationed at Central, in the heart of Sydney's central business district. Central, along with the then Darlinghurst Police Station, which was responsible for the red-light district of Kings Cross, were two of the busiest stations in New South Wales.

The man in charge at Central was Inspector Merv Beck, who was to achieve a reputation for breaking up a string of illegal gambling dens within the city. The detectives he lead in his clampdown of organised crime were later referred to as 'Beck's Raiders'.

When Peter arrived at Central, Inspector Beck gave the new recruits a no-nonsense speech. 'Welcome to Central. There are two types of police here,' he told the eager newbies, 'those who are in the shit and have been sent here to be punished, and probationary constables. It's your job as probationary constables to keep away from those who have been in the shit and keep your noses clean ... Good luck'.

Listening to Inspector Beck, Peter couldn't help but wonder what he had got himself into. It must be remembered that the late 1970s was a very different era and the New South Wales Police Force was a very different force. While there were officers such as Inspector Beck who upheld the law, it was also a time when some officers, such as the infamous Roger Rogerson, known as 'The Dodger', abused their powers for their own ends.

Despite the ominous welcome, Peter enjoyed being at Central. Obviously, as with any occupation, there were good times and bad times, but it was an eye-opener and he learned a lot every day. Even the long trip travelling into the city from Green Valley became easier as his enthusiasm for the job grew.

At the end of his probation, Peter was told he would be assigned to the Criminal Correspondence Branch, which prepared interstate summonses, traffic fines, and other legal notices in support of operational police. While this is important work that keeps the wheels of justice turning, it wasn't what Peter had joined to do. He wanted to be on the street, helping people, not stuck in an office shuffling papers. Not sure how he could get out of the assignment, Peter spoke to an officer he admired, Detective Senior Sergeant Joe Parrington. Detective Parrington, who looked like American actor Lee Marvin, was a gruff, old-school policeman. In 1977 he received a lot of media attention as one of the senior officers involved in the inquiry into the disappearance and murder of anti-drugs campaigner Donald MacKay in Griffith, western New South Wales.

When Peter explained his predicament—that he wanted to be a detective but was being sent to work in

Criminal Correspondence—the detective senior sergeant responded quite categorically, 'Well son, don't you worry about that. I'll fix that. You're a detective, and you'll be staying with me.'

Whatever it was that Senior Sergeant Parrington did, it worked. Peter began his career as a plain-clothes detective. He remained at Central for a couple more years before being transferred to Fairfield in Sydney's west. His time at Fairfield was short, just a few months, before he was transferred back into Sydney, where he took up a position at Newtown Police Station in Sydney's inner west. Such was the transient life of a young detective.

During Peter's time at Newtown a circular went around inviting detectives to consider a change of lifestyle and to apply for postings in rural centres. Peter was tempted. His mother had come from the country and, having only ever known the suburbs and city of Sydney, he was keen to see what a country life would be like, at least to give it a go for a couple of years, he thought. Peter put in his application for transfer and waited to see what he would be offered. He received his call. It was from Joe Parrington, who was then promoted to superintendent in charge of country transfers.

Superintendent Parrington said he had a country position for Peter and asked whether he would like to go to Bourke. The young detective was hesitant. Known as the gateway to the outback, located in far northwest New South Wales, Bourke was a little too far for Peter. He declined the offer. When he put down the receiver,

Peter was sure he had blown his chances and would never be offered a country posting again. Parrington thought differently, and a few weeks later called Peter again.

'I've got a position in Cessnock,' the gravel voice informed Peter.

'Where's Cessnock?'

'Near Maitland. Do you want it or not?' Parrington was not one for small talk, or to try to sell the proposition. He just wanted an answer.

Peter had heard of Maitland and knew that the Hunter region was only a few hours away from Sydney and his parents. He accepted.

In April 1983, five years after joining the New South Wales Police Force, Peter Fox walked into Cessnock Police Station's Criminal Investigation Branch. There, he met two detectives who he would admire as professionals and as friends. They were Ken Sneddon and Dave Woolnough. Both men would leave Peter with a lasting impression of what a detective should be and how they should conduct their work. Peter describes them as being, 'two of the most ethical, competent, and professional detectives I have ever had the pleasure to work with'.

Ken Sneddon, who sported a shock of white hair, demonstrated to Peter how to interview suspects. This father-like figure showed Peter how using tact and displaying an amount of empathy with the offender could get results. He believed in the old adage, 'You catch more flies with vinegar than honey'.

Even though he had worked on a few child sex cases by this time, Peter had yet to hear any paedophile admit to their crimes. They just wouldn't do it. They preferred to fight it out in court. Sitting in an interview with Ken Sneddon and their suspect, Peter was amazed at how the senior detective, by speaking calmly and in a fatherly manner, was able to gain the trust of the suspect who eventually broke down and confessed to his crime. Some offenders even became tearful as they admitted they had a 'disease' and needed help. And it didn't just happened once; Sneddon was successful numerous times. Peter realised then that this was how an interview should be conducted. There was no need for shouting and slapping the desk in frustration, as some did.

Because of Ken Sneddon's success rate in getting criminals to admit to their crimes, a saying was adopted among staff at the station. Whenever a confession was obtained during an interview it was known as a 'Sneddo', or, to use the verb, they'd say a criminal had been 'Sneddoed'.

Before arriving at Cessnock, Peter had always thought that Sydney was where it all happened and would prove to be the better training ground. At Cessnock, he discovered he was expected to do everything, including the tasks normally reserved for a more experienced detective. In short, he was thrown into the deep end. It was a steep learning curve for Peter, more because of the fact that Cessnock, as with other regional areas, has fewer detectives. Peter learned a lot in a very short time.

While working at Newtown, Peter was one of around twenty detectives, whereas when he arrived in Cessnock he was one of three. Although there was less crime being committed in country towns compared with the city, Peter still found his workload had increased fivefold, solely because of the lack of manpower. Also, whereas he was used to working with other detectives on jobs and sharing the tasks required, in Cessnock he found himself operating alone. Peter found this quite daunting in his early days, as he was relatively inexperienced in some facets of the job.

Peter's first afterhours callout was in response to a break and enter. Uniform police had caught four youths in the act at two in the morning. It seemed straightforward, but when it came time to transcribe the offenders' interviews on a typewriter, Peter realised he had never done this before. He phoned Ken Sneddon for guidance. Detective Sneddon replied, 'Foxy, I have every confidence in the world in you ... mate, this is when you work out for yourself whether you sink or swim, so start throwing your arms'.

Peter got through that night. There were more nights like this to follow, as result of which Peter found himself gaining more and more confidence in himself as an investigator. As his time at Cessnock went on, he was thankful for having made the move; the experience was proving invaluable.

Two other lessons Peter would learn in those early days were to be careful and to think clearly before jumping into a situation. On another occasion, Peter was again dragged from his sleep to be told there had been an armed robbery at Cessnock. There were four offenders and the victim was able to give police a description of the getaway car. Driving to the location, Peter spotted the wanted vehicle heading in the opposite direction. He quickly turned his car around and gave chase. The chase wasn't long: to Peter's amazement, the suspects willingly pulled over. Peter stepped out of his police vehicle with his gun, a standard issue .38 six-shooter Smith & Wesson revolver, pointed at the getaway car. He ordered the occupants out of the vehicle and told them to lie on the ground. Without any objection the four offenders obeyed his instructions. Peter took a quick look inside the car to make sure no one else was hiding between the seats. What he found, under the driver's seat, was the bag of cash and two sawn-off shotguns.

Peter had arrested four armed offenders on his own. Adrenalin had driven him to give chase and pull the robbers over. It had also clouded his judgment, to the point that he knew he was chasing four armed offenders but hadn't realised the risk he was taking. The problem Peter had was that any backup heading his way was, at best, half an hour away. It wasn't until shortly after seeing the shotguns that Peter realised what he had done and thought to himself, How bloody stupid am I?

Even so, Peter knew he had to give chase. He couldn't let the suspects escape, and besides, being on your own is just something that happens in the country. Had the offenders resisted with force Peter wouldn't have stood a chance. He admits he learned a valuable lesson that night, which, thankfully, wasn't a costly one. Luck was definitely smiling down on him that evening.

The country lifestyle suited Peter. He met a local girl whom he married. In 1990, Peter Fox led the District Drug Squad, then, after a couple of years in that position joined the detectives at Maitland, and then moved on to Singleton where he was an acting detective sergeant before finally returning to Cessnock with a promotion to detective sergeant.

In 1998 the New South Wales Police Service, as it was then known, was restructured under Commissioner Peter Ryan. There were three detectives' offices operating in the lower Hunter: Raymond Terrace, Cessnock and Maitland. The two former branches were closed and all the detectives were brought together at Maitland, which became the central office for the lower Hunter region.

During Peter's time in the Hunter he had made a reputation for himself as an officer who had compassion and empathy with victims, and a thoroughness and dedication to getting the work done. He is known for not giving up, even after exhausting every avenue of an investigation. In Peter's mind, there's always something else that can be done. He rarely stops thinking about a case. Even when he's at home relaxing, he will take out his notepad and jot down points to attend to back at work.

At the time he was investigating Judith Brown's murder, Peter and his wife were building a new home.

Often, Peter would be seen, sometimes to his wife's mild annoyance, hammering away, and then suddenly stopping to make notes for himself. Whether he was on the roof, out in the backyard, inside the house, or watching television, Peter couldn't switch off his mind. He couldn't leave Judith's family, or for that matter, any of the families from other cases, without some type of resolution. It would never bring Judith back, but at least it would give the family a feeling that her death mattered to police and, hopefully, that justice would be served.

Peter is also seen as being modest. He wouldn't accept that he had earned his reputation for himself, but rather was just continuing the example set him by his mentors from Cessnock, Ken Sneddon and Dave Woolnough.

Often, when addressing new detectives, Peter tells them they won't learn all there is to policing and interviewing from books and courses. The best way to learn, Peter explains, is to keep close, watch, and listen to experienced officers in the field. There's no better teacher.

～

After it had been established that Ross did not purchase any bottles of beer on the afternoon of Judith's murder he became the prime suspect. But if, as Peter now strongly suspected, Ross had killed his wife and was attempting to cover his tracks, there was still a lot of work to be done to prove it.

Other than Ross, the only witness to whether Ross might have committed murder was Floyd the

Staffordshire terrier, and he wasn't going to be much help. Peter needed to speak further with Ross's friends and associates at Singleton. Not that there was anything to indicate they would have any useful information, but Peter considered it worthwhile because he could learn how Ross had been behaving since the murder and what he had been telling people.

Peter was still waiting on the results of the physical evidence sent to the Analytical Laboratories, hoping it might help support his theory or even reveal something to identify the killer. He was anxious to hear, too, from the banks on the Browns' financial situation. If Ross was the killer, Peter knew he would have to find a motive and put together enough evidence to support what would most likely be a circumstantial case, in which pieces of information, when put together infer certain facts without any evidence linking Ross directly to the murder. After all, there were no witnesses who saw Ross commit the murder, or anyone that could place him in the house at precisely 9.14.28.

At this time, Peter shared his suspicions and theories with some of his colleagues. While they agreed that Ross was most likely responsible for the murder, they didn't believe Peter would be able to gather enough evidence, circumstantial or otherwise, against him. Even if he did, there were those who were sceptical that the brief of evidence would stand up in a court. They felt it would be difficult to prove Ross's guilt beyond a reasonable doubt to a magistrate at a committal hearing, or, if it went to trial, to a jury.

Despite advice to the contrary, Peter decided to go ahead. He believed there was more to be known and he wanted to follow it through, no matter how it turned out.

Chapter 7

MISSING MONEY AND ODD BEHAVIOUR

Following the walk-through, which had been conducted on Tuesday 6 June, Ross returned to Singleton. He and his three boys stayed with Murray and Sally before eventually moving into a rental property in Wilcox Avenue, Singleton Heights. The house was furnished with the possessions from the Clonmeen Circuit house.

Looking into Ross and Judith's finances, Peter Fox learned that from what remained of the proceeds of selling their home in Gardener Circuit in Singleton, together with Ross's redundancy payment, the couple, after paying off debts such as car loans and the like, had placed $35 000 in a fixed term deposit. The account was originally in both their names, but in September 1999 the bank received a request and marked the fixed term deposit 'to be in Judy's name only'. There was a second account, which remained in both names, that held the remaining funds and was used to purchase new furnishings when the family moved to Anna Bay in January 2000.

On 7 April 2000, Ross sold his house at Tanilba Bay for $95 000. One week later he withdrew $80 000 and deposited it into the fixed term account, bringing the total in that account to $117 847.68, which included interest already paid on the $35 000. The account remained in Judith's name.

The rest of the money, around $15 000, was put into one of two joint building society accounts the couple had set up. The second account was where Judith's wages were being paid into. Within six weeks $12 180.45 over nineteen transactions had been withdrawn from the first account. The bank confirmed seventeen of these transactions had been made personally by Ross. The bank could not confirm whether Ross or Judith had made the additional two withdrawals. By the end of May that same year the account was completely emptied.

Peter learned that an incident occurred at the Anna Bay Tavern involving a declined EFTPOS transaction some time during May. Ross had tried to take out some money, only to learn he had insufficient funds. One of the patrons at the Tavern remembered Ross telling him, 'There's been a stuff up at the bank. I won $80 000 on Lotto and I've been waiting for the money to come in.'

Peter assumed Ross was referring to the $80 000 he had placed in the fixed term deposit. There had been no mention of a Lotto win to police by Ross or by anyone who knew him.

On 31 May, Ross phoned the real estate agent managing the Clonmeen Circuit house about the due rent. This was the first time he had been unable to pay the rent on time. He promised the agency he would pay the $380 the following day, but failed to do so. That same day, Ross also contacted his bank and ordered a replacement Visa credit card. When the bank enquired what had happened to the old card, Ross replied, 'It has been thrown in the garbage'.

On Thursday 1 June, the day before Judith's murder, Ross phoned his bank again. He spoke to the manager. 'We have a term deposit just in my wife's name. How can we put the deposit into joint names, because there's some funny business going on, if you know what I mean?'

The manager explained that Ross and Judith would have to fill out some forms and that the transfer of names could take a week to ten days. Ross never elaborated on what he meant by 'funny business'.

According to people Judith had spoken to during May, she had mentioned she was eager to purchase a new home and that she was concerned about the family finances. She said they were using their savings and she was finding it hard to make ends meet. Optimistically, though, she told relatives that she had put some money away, that 'there is $130 000 and nobody is going to get that … that is for our house'.

Studying the accounts, Peter believed Judith was adding the amount in the fixed term deposit—$117 847.68—to the money in the joint account to arrive at the $130 000. It was the only explanation for having reached the specified total. If this was so, then Judith was, at the time of her call to her family, obviously unaware of the depletion of the money in the joint account.

Peter Fox also learnt that Ross, since returning to Singleton, had by the end of July, sold Judith's green Daewoo Numira hatchback for $10 000 and was receiving income from social security as well as having been given money from various community groups.

Due to the popularity of and fondness for Judith and the Brown family within the Singleton community, a group of women ran a raffle to raise money for the three boys. A total of $1055.00 was raised. Ross received a further $1560.50 from other sources.

As far as Peter knew Ross hadn't yet been granted access to any of Judith's money, so the $117 847.68 remained in the fixed term deposit. With Judith as the sole signatory Ross hadn't been able to get a hold of the money, despite applying for probate, the legal process of validating a Will and appointing an executor who then distributes the proceeds of the estate after settling any outstanding obligations.

The reason why Ross hadn't received official permission to access Judith's account was unclear, but most likely it was just a normal delay, part of the bureaucracy of the Supreme Court. Thus it was surprising to Peter when he learned of Judith's car being sold. The car was part of Judith's estate, and Ross had no legal right to dispose of that asset at that time.

Ross's spending habits were also a concern for Peter. Of the money Ross had accumulated during July, a total of $12 615.15, little of it remained in any of the joint accounts shared by Ross and Judith. At the end of August the two building society accounts were showing a balance of just $9.11 and $4.16.

Peter didn't know where the money had gone, whether Ross was transferring it into another account that the police were not aware of, if he had been buying lavish household items, or just squandering it on himself and his three boys. Wherever it was, whatever it had been spent on, Peter knew he needed to speak with Ross's friends again. He hoped they might provide an insight into Ross that might or might not confirm his suspicions.

⟶

Peter noted a marked change in Ross and Judith's friends when he asked if he could speak with them again. When police initially approached them, it was only days after Judith's murder and most were in shock at the news. They either didn't want to talk, were unable to talk, or didn't feel they had anything to contribute. With time, the friends had dealt with their grief and were doing what they could for Ross and the boys. Some helped with the move from Anna Bay, some loaned Ross money, others just lent a sympathetic ear.

Several people urged Ross to seek counselling for himself and his children. One of his son's teachers also tried to convince Ross of the value of speaking with a professional grief counsellor. Ross refused. He would become angry and defiant at the suggestion. He even confronted one of his sons in the playground after speaking with his teacher. In front of all the other children Ross asked his son if he wanted to see a counsellor. The son declined. Ross strode up to the teacher and said, 'There, I've asked him again and he doesn't want counselling.'

The teacher was deeply hurt by the incident and also

felt that Ross's son was embarrassed, but in this respect, there was nothing anyone could do.

As the months passed, friends were beginning to develop their own opinions of Ross and whether he was involved in Judith's murder. Those whom Peter approached agreed to speak with him. There were others who contacted Peter directly, eager to speak to police about their concerns. From all the people Peter spoke to, one message was very clear: they all suspected that Ross had killed Judith.

Some friends based their suspicions on the fact that, since her death, Ross never spoke about Judith, that he appeared to be behaving as though she had never existed. This observation struck a chord with Peter. The only interaction the detectives had with him was on the Friday of the murder and the following Tuesday during the walk-through. In all his years as a detective and in all the cases he had been involved in, he couldn't think of an instance where a close friend, a relative, or, especially, the spouse of a victim, didn't call for an update on the investigation. It was a very common occurrence for those close to the victim to want to know that the police were still doing their job. They wanted justice. They wanted closure. In contrast, Ross never called Peter Fox or any other police involved in the investigation.

Peter was told that when Ross returned to Singleton after the day of the walk-through he went for a drink with Murray, who he was staying with at the time, and a couple of other mutual friends at a local club. As the night wore on Ross asked Murray to tell his three boys and members of Judith's family that the police didn't suspect him of Judith's murder. Perhaps he thought this news would be better coming from a friend.

While the request seemed odd, Murray later complied and passed the word around. One of the other friends at the club that night then told Murray that after Ross had asked him to spread the word, the friend saw Ross jumping up, punching the air and, in an elated tone, let out a 'Yes', repeating the word over and over.

There had always been a question in Peter's mind as to why Ross would leave his highly-paid job working at the open cut mine to move to Anna Bay. Ross had just said Judith and he wanted a change. Yet the first thing Ross did after Judith's murder was to move back to Singleton.

Admittedly, the move back wasn't seen as being anything other than Ross wanting to be around the people he knew best, to be where he and his sons would receive strong emotional support. The question still remained, however, why leave the security of the mine?

Most likely people were more open with Peter than they had been earlier because of their own suspicions. Peter learnt from them that Ross was known for taking illegal drugs and, the friends believed, Judith wanted to get him away from Singleton to try to sever his association with dealers and possibly other users. She wanted him to clean up his act.

There was also the fact that the management at Howick open cut mine had initiated increased drug testing and this, according to friends, concerned Ross. Without Ross having admitted to any of this, Peter viewed the information for what it was—pure speculation.

The women who had organised the raffle had an interesting story to tell. They decided to run the raffle to help the three boys. The money they raised from it would be used for school needs or to assist with their rugby league. They knew Ross's reputation with money and didn't want him getting his hands on it, so, even though they didn't tell him about the raffle, it wasn't long before he became aware of the money. He demanded the women hand over the cash; they refused. After some argument, a compromise was reached and the money was given to a mutual friend. Ross still wanted the money. To alleviate the situation, the friend had Ross give him a list of bills that needed to be paid. The friend then used the proceeds of the raffle to pay the monies owed. Not quite what the women had wanted; they had arranged the raffle so the money could go to the boys.

Despite his friends' attempts to help him and his three sons Ross was obviously not endearing himself to people. What Peter learned was that the people who had gathered around to offer their support counted themselves as friends of Judith rather than Ross. It seemed Judith was the reason they had got to know Ross. Of all the people Peter spoke to, there wasn't anyone who would say they were Ross's friend.

It didn't surprise Peter that Ross appeared not to

have any close friends. Certainly, what Peter had experienced of Ross's behaviour told him he was a very volatile type of person, and someone who preferred to keep to himself. Offers of help or advice would not have been welcomed.

Ross's violent and erratic behaviour on the Friday afternoon of Judith's murder and his emotionally dissociated and peculiar display on the Tuesday of the walk-through were still of concern to Peter. He couldn't be sure if Ross was just being himself or whether his actions revealed something deeper. Was Ross's behaviour betraying him as the killer?

Being a policeman, Peter had been exposed to a number of diverse personalities from all walks of life, some bad and some good. Through the years he and his colleagues had developed natural instincts that enabled them to know when they were being lied too, and when they weren't being told the whole truth. It had nothing to do with supernatural abilities, or believing that everyone lies, but with close observation of a suspect's body language, avoiding eye contact, the inflection of their voice, and other subtle telltale signs.

While Peter's suspicions of Ross's actions were based on his experience with people in similar circumstances, he still couldn't be 100 per cent sure. Even if he were right, no court would accept his observations as he wasn't a qualified psychologist. He needed to test his suspicions, to know if Ross's behaviour, particularly on the Friday afternoon, was an elaborate act concocted to try to conceal his guilt. To find out, Peter turned to

Doctor Michael Diamond, a forensic psychologist.

This wasn't an easy decision for Peter to make. As it does for the examinations of the physical evidence collected from the crime scene and other places, employing the skills of a forensic psychologist costs money. This meant Peter had to convince his superiors that such a task would be beneficial to the investigation. Based on Peter's own observations and the evidence to date, management agreed and Dr Diamond was commissioned to conduct his study.

～⌒

Dr Michael Diamond is a highly respected psychologist, a member of the Australian and New Zealand Association of Psychotherapy, and one of a number of psychologists New South Wales Police use to try and get into the mind of suspects. In order to be able to make his assessment, Dr Diamond requires a mountain of information.

Peter provided the doctor with transcripts and copies of the videotapes taken during the Friday evening interview and the Tuesday walk-through with Ross. In addition, Peter handed over copies of statements made by relatives and friends, giving as comprehensively as possible a background on Ross and Judith's time together, as well as the autopsy report and video and photos of the crime scene. As with profiling, a lot can be deduced about an offender by examining the injuries suffered by the victim.

Looking through the report and visual material of the crime scene and autopsy, Dr Diamond believed

Judith knew her killer and would have felt safe and secure in his or her company. Even if she had been in an argument with the person, she would not have thought her life was in danger. The attack on her person would have come as a complete surprise.

In Dr Diamond's words:

... the fact she was so utterly surprised and made very little defensive movement is suggestive that her attacker was someone with who she felt comfortable and familiar ... the fact that the supposed murder weapon and location of her body were virtually adjacent to each other further suggests that what happened occurred suddenly and with great rage.

Reading through the witness statements from neighbours who recounted Ross's behaviour immediately after discovering Judith's body on the Friday afternoon, Dr Diamond found Ross to be, 'highly abnormal and dramatic'. He also noted that 'the content of his speech was repetitive and emphatic'.

Viewing the video of Ross's interview with Peter Fox and Graeme Parker on the night of the murder, Dr Diamond pointed out that at no time during the lengthy interview did Ross state he was too upset or emotional to continue. Having to talk about Judith, their relationship together, and going over the events leading to the discovery of his wife's body, Dr Diamond would have expected Ross to have been overcome with grief. It would have been a natural reaction to losing a loved one so suddenly and unexpectedly.

While Dr Diamond believed that Ross 'does not show

emotion which might be consistent with a bereft and stunned individual', he also noted that Ross was offered opportunities to suspend the interview but declined. Ross stated that he wanted to 'get it over and done with'. For Dr Diamond, this again is in conflict with a husband having lost his spouse in tragic circumstances.

Dr Diamond found Ross's demeanour throughout the interview was one of 'irritation and anger', not anguish and sorrow. Referring to Judith in terms such as 'I come home to this' and 'what a fuckin' mess' only confirmed Dr Diamond's summation that Ross's behaviour 'is difficult to reconcile with someone who may be grief-stricken or overwhelmed'.

Dr Diamond also believed that the cut to Ross's left hand was not accidental. It was, most likely, self-inflicted, possibly as a ploy to gain sympathy and for Ross to appear to be the victim.

During the walk-through, Dr Diamond noted, only days after the murder, Ross again showed no emotion as he took police through the house and stepped over the exact spot where Judith's body had lain. Although Ross was in the house where he had encountered the grotesque sight of his wife's battered body, he seemed more concerned with giving police details of his movements. Ross's emotional state appeared to change little throughout the day.

The report from Dr Diamond confirmed all Peter Fox had suspected: Ross had put on a performance on the Friday afternoon, and he felt little, if any, emotion over the death of his wife. This meant Ross was trying to hide his guilt for killing Judith. All well and good, but how did it help Peter? After all, he couldn't arrest Ross just on the basis of his erratic and suspicious behaviour.

Dr Diamond did give Peter some advice on how to tackle his problem. During his time assessing Ross, he noticed that Ross had a great respect for his father and paternal grandfather. He saw them as men's men, and quite possibly modelled himself after them. He held them in high esteem. Given this, Dr Diamond believed that Ross would treat any father figure in a similar manner as he would his own relations. If Ross were to be confronted with his crime by a father figure, he might just realise his guilt, break down, and confess. There were no guarantees, but Dr Diamond felt it was Peter's best chance at getting Ross to admit to the murder.

Peter decided to follow Dr Diamond's advice. The evidence against Ross remained limited; there was not enough there to satisfy Peter's superiors or the Director of Public Prosecutions (DPP). Results from the physical evidence collected by Peter Muscio and the other crime scene investigators came in around this time. Unfortunately, the results didn't point directly to Ross being the offender, but they did raise more questions about the crime scene, in particular: Was there any evidence to show anyone other than Ross could have killed Judith?

Blood found in the house, on the handle of the rear sliding door, the tiled floor, the wall, the carpet, the broken bottles, and the piece of ceramic that had adhered to the bedroom carpet, was consistent with belonging to either Judith or Ross. The blood found on the leather cover of the gearstick in Ross's Toyota was too contaminated to give a match. The rubber pedal covers removed from the clutch, brake, and accelerator of Ross's four-wheel-drive all returned a negative for any presence of blood. No ceramic, paint flakes, or fine glass fragments were located in the cabin. The bloodstained shoeprints found around the house were matched to Ross's shoes, which he had worn on the day.

While the findings were as expected, it did rule out the likelihood of a second person having been in the house to commit the murder. However careful an unknown assailant might have been, the attack was so violent that they could not have avoided leaving some trace evidence behind at the scene. Police would have expected one of the shoeprints to belong to a third party, or even a trace or smudge of Judith's blood leading out onto the back patio, given it would have been the most likely entrance and exit.

There was also the fact that, based on the weight of the statue and it being used repeatedly, the offender would have been covered in Judith's blood. This lead Peter back to Joel's statement that he had seen his father wearing a flannel shirt and black tracksuit pants on the Friday morning, different to the apparel he wore in the afternoon. Was the wet flannel shirt found in the second laundry basket an attempt by Ross to wash away incriminating evidence?

Peter Muscio from Crime Scene had inspected the shirt on the Monday after the murder. He had a good look at it, along with other clothing in both baskets, but couldn't see any obvious signs of blood. Peter discussed with other colleagues whether any of the clothing should be collected, but at the time, everyone agreed they had enough items to examine.

By Monday 5 June, police weren't sure Ross would become a suspect. They also had no information that would lead them to think that Ross had changed clothing, or that he had worn the grey flannel shirt. With over 120 other pieces of physical evidence to sort through, all the clothing was left and would eventually be returned to Ross.

Peter Fox now had a list of questions he needed to put to Ross. Even though Peter could continue his investigation without involving his suspect, he wanted to know how Ross could explain the obvious inconsistencies in his statement. He wanted to know what Ross would have to say when confronted with the evidence that showed he hadn't purchased the two beer bottles. What would be his reaction to the witness who saw his vehicle in the driveway after nine o'clock on the morning of the murder? Why did Ross drink in excess of twelve schooners at the Tavern when he had to take one of his sons to rugby league practice that afternoon? And could Ross explain the damp grey flannel shirt in the washing basket or the circular stain on the partition?

The interview would serve two purposes. First, it was hoped that by confronting Ross with his lies and showing how the evidence had narrowed to him as the only suspect, he just might confess. The second purpose, should Ross not confess, would be to get him to commit to whatever answers he gave. Not having any forewarning of what police had discovered meant Ross would either be forced into telling the truth or he would have to tell an outright lie to try and cover for himself. Either way, Peter would have on tape and in black and white all of Ross's responses to the evidence.

Waiting to gather more evidence so as to arrest Ross could possibly tip Peter's hand and give Ross time to think up creative explanations that might be difficult for police to disprove. Peter couldn't afford to give Ross any opportunity to cover his tracks.

While Peter and his superiors agreed it was necessary to speak with Ross a third time, Ross was not under any obligation to take part in a third interview. Peter felt that if he asked, Ross would most likely refuse, particularly if he believed he was a suspect. He needed a good reason for getting Ross back in. It didn't take Peter long to find his excuse; it was sitting in the evidence room of Maitland Police Station.

Chapter 8

MOUNTING EVIDENCE

Some time around late August or early September, Peter Fox received a report from Suzanne Breeze, an analyst at the Analytical Laboratory in Lidcombe. Suzanne had been studying the piece of ceramic found in the main bedroom, which had been glued to the carpet. Using the statue handed in to police, it was possible to identify the broken piece as being a portion of the swag, the sleeping bag slung over the back of the swagman. The fragment was covered in Judith's blood, transported somehow by the assailant to the entrance of the bedroom, where it lay. While resting, the blood dried, which explained how it became adhered to the fibres of the carpet. On closer examination, Suzanne found, as Peter Muscio had first noticed, that the blood had also enveloped a small sliver of glass consistent with the type of glass used to make beer bottles.

The sliver of glass was studied further and eventually found to be consistent with the glass from the long-necked bottles of beer found shattered in the foyer. The ceramic fragment itself had sharp edges and a clean inside surface, indicating it had recently been broken from the main statue. In other words, the fragment had been broken during the murder and not previously.

This was important, as police might have needed to establish if the broken piece of ceramic was a recent break, or a piece lying about the house from an earlier incident. Ross might argue in his defence that the fragment had been broken off the statue well before the day of the murder and that the sliver of glass had become embedded in the ceramic from an earlier time, that he had dropped a bottle of beer some time previous to the day of the murder, and that the glass sliver must have rested on the ceramic. Therefore, to eliminate such an excuse, it was crucial for police to establish the most likely time when the fragment cracked away from the statue. But what evidence did police have to tell them that the glass sliver came in contact with the ceramic at the time of the murder and not after?

The glass sliver was found on the inside surface of the ceramic, the area that had broken away. When Peter Muscio and his team of crime scene examiners discovered the piece on the night of the murder, the fragment of ceramic was found with the outer surface, the glazed painted area, facing down onto the carpet. The inside surface was facing up, and the sliver was covered in blood. For the sliver of beer bottle glass to be found on the ceramic and under the dried blood, the only possible explanation was that the glass had met with the ceramic after it broke away from the statue.

As the statue was being used in the attack, this meant that the piece of ceramic broke away, fell into the growing pool of blood on the floor of the foyer, and met with a sliver of beer bottle glass. The two, immersed in the blood, then came together. At some point, the ceramic became transferred to the bedroom, where the blood dried, became glued to the fibres and enveloped the sliver. The drying of the blood refuted any suggestion that the sliver might have been transferred to the ceramic during the afternoon of the murder.

Analyst Suzanne Breeze had provided Peter Fox with the physical evidence to support his theory that at least one beer bottle had been broken on the morning of the murder, possibly at the time the murder was being committed. Peter discussed the evidence with his colleagues, crime scene investigators and forensic analysts. While it was a strong piece of circumstantial evidence and created great excitement among fellow detectives, it still wasn't enough for Peter to go ahead and arrest Ross. Although his brief of evidence was growing, it wasn't yet strong enough to convince a jury. Peter needed more.

～

The third interview with Ross Brown was considered the most crucial of all for Peter Fox. It was during this interview that Peter would present Ross, for the first time, with the evidence that had been gathered, which pointed to him as being Judith's killer. Peter didn't want anything to go wrong. He wanted to be sure before bringing Ross in that the interview would go according to plan and that all contingencies were covered.

Following advice from Dr Michael Diamond, Peter decided to introduce Ross to a father figure, thereby hoping to help Ross admit to his guilt. Peter couldn't take on the role, as he and Ross were close in age, so Peter turned to Detective Sergeant Alex Pollock. Peter knew Alex well and had a lot of respect for him as a policeman and as an interrogator. Alex was close to retirement and, at that time, was filling in as acting crime manager at Muswellbrook Police Station in the Upper Hunter. When Peter approached him and explained the role he was to play during the interview, Alec agreed to help out.

Peter furnished Alex with the videotapes and transcripts from the first two interviews with Ross, the one taken on the evening of the murder, the other at the walk-through. Alex was also given photos from the crime scene, the autopsy report, statements from neighbours, relatives and friends, and lab results of the physical evidence sent to Lidcombe. Peter wanted Alex to be fully briefed on the whole of the investigation.

As Alex would be the father figure, the interview strategy was kept simple. They weren't going to play good cop, bad cop. Instead, Peter would put the evidence collected since the murder to Ross. Alex would observe, listening to Ross's answers. Then, if Ross refused to accept the evidence and stuck to his story Alex, when he felt the moment was right, would engage Ross and speak to him man to man. Pete hoped Alex might appeal to Ross's conscience and be able to extract a confession.

Peter decided to prepare a contingency plan should the strategy not work. With approval from his superiors and a judge's signature on the warrants, Peter had a listening device at his disposal.

Murray, who already had his own suspicions by this time, agreed to assist Peter and would wear the listening device. It was arranged that, as before, Murray would accompany Ross to Maitland Police Station for the interview. This time, however, Murray would be fitted with the listening device and, during their return to Singleton, start asking Ross a lot of questions about the interview in the hope Ross might, in a careless moment, say something incriminating.

Whatever the outcome of the interview, Peter didn't want to miss any opportunity that might help towards solving the case.

The other situation, of course, was how to get Ross into the interview room. The solution to the problem was quickly found when Peter realised he still had the marijuana and bong, the illegal drug and smoking device, in the evidence room. Ross hadn't been charged with possession of an illegal substance at the time Peter and Graeme Parker found the drug in the Clonmeen Circuit house on Tuesday 6 June. Now, with Ross as the prime suspect, Peter decided to use the find as the excuse to get Ross in.

Peter contacted Ross and told him he needed to see him for the outstanding matter involving the drugs they found during the walk-through. He explained to Ross that he couldn't ignore finding the drugs and that they would have to charge him. Ross was understanding and agreed to meet with Peter at Maitland Police station. Peter also told him he wanted to talk further about

Judith's murder and to clear up a few things that had come to his notice, developments in the investigation.

As arranged, Ross drove from Singleton to Maitland Police Station with Murray in tow. The two men walked into the station at around ten o'clock on the morning of 10 October 2000. Ross Brown was taken to the charge room and formally charged with possession of an illegal substance. For Ross to be charged he first had to be arrested and placed in custody. Being in custody gave Peter and Alex Pollock the right to question Ross on any matter they believed he could assist with, namely Judith's murder.

The charge officer arranged for Ross to appear before the Magistrates' Court a couple of weeks later to answer the possession charge. With Ross still technically in custody, and once the earlier formalities had been finalised, Peter took Ross to the interview room where he and Alex Pollock began their interrogation.

The interview began at 10.32 a.m. Ross was quite friendly and comfortable with the two detectives, despite having just been charged. His demeanour was the same as it had been when he conducted the walk-through. He treated Peter and the new detective, Alex, like friends, referring to them by their first names and as 'mate'.

The first point Peter raised with Ross was the small sliver of glass found on the broken piece of ceramic. He showed Ross photos of the fragment, explaining it had come from the statue and was located just inside the main bedroom. Peter pointed out the tiny piece of glass, telling Ross that 'The blood seems to have glued that piece of beer glass to that portion of the statue ... Can you explain how that may have occurred? Do you have any idea?'

'No, I don't, Peter, I don't,' Ross replied, adding, 'I had bottles of beer in my hand when I went home that day.'

Peter admitted that this physical evidence puzzled police, particularly as Ross claims to have broken the beer bottles in the afternoon. 'We can't understand how a piece of broken glass is actually stuck in the blood,' inferring that this must have happened at the time of the murder.

Ross accepted the evidence, but didn't change his story. 'Peter, I can't answer that. I've got no idea, mate. I know I came home that day and I had some beer bottles, bottles of beer, um ...'

Nothing was going to be achieved by pushing the point, so Peter changed tack. He wanted to establish the time Ross left the house on the Friday morning. In the previous interviews Ross claimed he had left at about 8.00 to drive his eldest son Riley to school. Riley began school at 8.30 a.m. Ross then returned home at around 8.15, in time to see his two younger sons off to school. Joel and Gene left at approximately 8.40. Ross said he then set off for the beach, just before 9.00.

It was then put to Ross that a neighbour, Danni, gave a statement to say she saw his car in the driveway at about 9.10 a.m. on the Friday morning. Was it possible Ross had not left until after 9.00 a.m?

'I can't answer that at all, Peter, because I'm pretty sure I was down the garage, umm, between 9.00 and ten past.' Ross was referring to the service station from which he said he had purchased $10 or $15 worth of diesel.

Peter read Danni's statement, how she always left for work between ten past and twenty past, and stressed to Ross that he believed she was certain of the time as she checked her clock before she went to her front door.

Ross said he checked his watch, though he admitted he wasn't sure how accurate it was, but he knew he was down at the service station between 9.00 and ten past.

'Is there any reason, um, you specifically remember … why you looked at your watch at that time, that morning?' Peter asked.

'Oh, not really, I, no, I can't say,' was Ross's response.

Ross was then asked if there was any appointment he had to keep to explain why he was at the garage getting fuel at that time, and why he left the house before 9.00.

'No, all I was doing, I was just going down to the beach like I usually do, take the dog down [sic].'

'Is it possible you might have left at ten past 9.00 or a little bit later?'

'No, not unless my watch is out of whack.'

Judith's watch became the next issue. Ross informed Peter and Alex that Judith had two watches, the one she wore on the day of her murder, and another that was a clip-on nurses' watch. She wore the latter when working at the retirement village and as an assistant nurse. Ross conceded that Judith would have kept both watches close to the exact time, though he couldn't be sure.

Ross was then shown a photograph of Judith's broken watch. Peter pointed out that it had stopped at 9.14.28. He also told Ross that police believed Judith's watch had stopped at the time she was being attacked. If this was correct, then the window of opportunity for someone to gain access to the house and commit the murder was very narrow. Whether Ross left the house just before 9.00 or at ten past, the murderer would have had between four and fourteen minutes.

Ross said he understood what Peter was explaining, but when asked if he had anything to say about this fact, Ross simply replied, 'No, I don't'.

Unlike popular police fiction, investigators interviewing a suspect don't become frustrated and thump desks until the suspect has given them the answer they seek. Rather, the suspect has the right to answer, to give a possible explanation of the evidence, say they don't know, or even to defer the question altogether. If the reply is one of the latter two options, then police move on to the next line of questioning. There's no advantage in bullying a suspect into giving an explanation.

Peter then touched on the blood discovered on the gearshift cover in his vehicle. The three boys had already told police back in June that their mother didn't like driving Ross's four-wheel-drive. She found it too heavy to manoeuvre. They also couldn't remember any time their mother might have injured herself and bled in the car. Ross agreed, though he did add that he cut himself at times when he took the family fishing. He would also be scratched and cut while playing with the dog, which he did all the time.

During the walk-through on Tuesday 6 June, Ross had told Peter and Graeme Parker that, after discovering his wife's body, he came back outside the house and might have leaned on his vehicle. He couldn't be sure whether he sat in the cabin of the Toyota, but Peter needed to establish if he had sat in it on the afternoon of the murder, to try and explain why blood was found on the gearshift. It was also more of a mystery as police had found the vehicle locked when they tried to gain access and Ross's keys were lying near Judith's body among the broken beer bottles.

'Peter, I've, I'll be honest with you, I've racked my brain and I still can't say yes or no. I didn't. That's the honest truth.'

Looking over the evidence showing the bloodied footprints and pawprints covering the inside of the house, police had established that Floyd, the Staffordshire terrier, had run through the blood to the back door, then to the interior door leading to the garage. Ross's blood and fingerprints were found on the handle and latch to the door, presumably the result of either letting the dog out or locking it after he had come back in. Ross's footprints, along with Floyd's prints, trailed to the main bedroom, then across the lounge room, where both become faint and required the use of Leuco Crystal Violet to highlight them.

Based on this physical evidence, it appeared that Ross, after discovering his wife, checked the bedroom and went and tended to his dog before raising the alarm. Peter put it to Ross. 'On the night I asked you why you didn't use your phone to make the triple 0 call and you couldn't really explain that to me, but what I am also curious about is, with your wife lying there, I would have thought you would have ran out immediately and tried to get help, but it appears that you've walked in here and you've, I'll put it bluntly, it just seems that you had more concern about letting the dog out of the house first and letting him go in the backyard than what you did running out and telling someone "Listen, somebody get some help".'

Ross couldn't remember 'running around the house'. He told the detectives he loved his wife, and if they cared to ask anyone, people would tell them how much he loved Judith and that he and Judith had never had an argument. If they did argue, it was over in the click of a finger.

In response to his movements through the house on the afternoon of the murder, Ross added, 'I don't even know if I've gone into shock after I found my wife, because I've never been in shock before, I don't know, mate. I honestly don't, um, I do believe that I was in shock throughout this, I don't, don't know actually what shock is because I've never been in that situation before.'

Going back over his statement, Ross again confirmed that he had purchased the two long-necked bottles of Toohey's New from the Anna Bay Tavern

Bottle Shop on the Friday afternoon. He clarified for Peter and Alex that he had offered a friend, Joe, a lift and as they set off Joe needed to buy a carton to take home. They went to Abb's Bottle Shop and after the purchase, Ross and Joe continued their journey until they saw a mutual friend they wanted to catch up with. Ross and Joe ended up back at the Tavern. Joe bought Ross a beer and then Ross decided to go to the Tavern's bottle shop where he claimed he bought the two bottles of Toohey's New. Once he had the bottles he left the Tavern and went straight home.

Peter wanted Ross to be sure of the events leading up to and including the purchase of the bottles. Ross was taken through his original statement carefully and asked again at which bottle shop he had bought the two long-necks.

Ross was adamant he had gone to the Anna Bay Tavern Bottle Shop, even when it was put to him that he could possibly have got them from the other bottle shop. After all, it was at Abb's Bottle Shop that Joe collected his carton of beer. Ross refuted the suggestion, though he admitted to having bought beer from both shops in the past.

When Peter explained he had the sales receipt and security video evidence that contradicted this, Ross appeared surprised and stated, 'I know this is a pretty serious thing and, well, if I didn't buy them there I must have got them at the other one … I'm sorry about that … I can't suggest any reason why I should hide buying a couple of bottles of beer.'

Again, the detectives presented the evidence refuting his claims that he purchased the bottles at Abb's Bottle Shop. Ross was even more taken aback. Peter observed Ross's reaction closely. He felt Ross was genuinely surprised at the length police had gone to check on his story. It was obvious to Peter that Ross had never imagined police would test his version of events.

Faced with the evidence Ross responded, 'Well, Christ, you've shocked me … I'll tell you now, I don't know what to say now, mate … I honestly don't … I was dead sure I bought them at the, the pub bottle shop … I was, I was absolutely sure I bought them there.'

Peter wondered if Ross was aware of the implication of the evidence. Ross was. 'This is very important and I, I was dead set sure I bought them at that bottle shop [the Tavern] and there's the only other, there's no other place around the area you can buy beer.'

Despite being presented with all the evidence, which clearly showed he had not purchased any bottles of beer from either bottle shop on the Friday afternoon, Ross dug in his heels and insisted he had. He repeated again that he had bought the two bottles from the Tavern's bottle shop. No amount of evidence would convince him otherwise, though he could not explain why there was no sales or visual record supporting his claim.

Naturally, the next question was, if Ross didn't buy the beers on that afternoon, how could he explain the broken glass in the foyer of the house?

Ross avoided giving a direct answer, but still insisted his recollection was correct. 'I was virtually a hundred percent sure I bought them at the pub at Anna Bay, okay? I was a hundred percent sure I bought at the pub at Anna Bay [sic]. There's nowhere else in Anna Bay that you can buy a beer, except them [sic] two places, and I'm sure, I was absolutely sure I got them at the pub and you can say you seen the videos and all that, um, ah, I've got no idea what to say, but I'm sure I got them at the pub at Anna Bay and I don't care about videos and all that, but that's where I'm saying I got that from.'

Even when Peter tried to move on from the bottle shops and concentrate on when Ross discovered his wife's body, Ross would interrupt the questioning, exploding in disbelief that there was no record of him buying beer at the Anna Bay Tavern Bottle Shop. 'I'm, I'm still in shock that I've just been told that I didn't purchased [sic] it at the pub, but I'm, I was absolutely positive I purchased them at the pub.'

Then, soon after, as Peter tried to steer the questioning to the round blood mark on top of the partition, Ross again interrupted with, 'I bought one, I don't know if I bought them over the bar, the whole pub is on video. The whole pub is on video.'

Ross's continued denial dumbfounded Peter and Alex. Ross had his story and he was sticking to it, regardless. Peter felt Ross believed he had got away with murder, and so long as he stuck to his version of events he'd be in the clear. But he had underestimated how thoroughly police would check his statement.

Peter displayed a series of photographs that clearly

showed the foyer area and the bloodstained ring on the top of the partition. Ross, though continuing to be mystified by the bottle shop evidence, still claimed that when he walked in and saw Judith on the ground he 'just dropped' the bottles of beer. Given this, could Ross explain how 'a ring of blood that is possibly from the bottom of a beer bottle' ended up on the partition?

'Like I said, I walked in, seen my wife there. Like I said, I, I don't know what's happened in this house after I walked in, I'm, I'm putting pictures together as best I can for you, um, like I said I thought I let them [bottles of beer] go and it's just like the bottle shop bit I was positive I bought them beer at the Anna Bay Bottle Shop, not the Anna Bay Hotel, the bottle shop. I was, I would bet my life on that.'

At this point, to help Ross keep track, Peter reviewed the evidence he had. There was the neighbour who saw Ross's vehicle in the driveway some time after 9.00, most likely at ten past, according to the neighbour's routine. Judith's watch, which showed she was attacked at around 9.14.28, indicated that an intruder had a very narrow window of opportunity— from when Ross claimed he left and Judith's watch stopping. There were Ross's movements throughout the house, as indicated by his footprints, which suggested he didn't go straight out to get help as he had told detectives earlier he had, blood on the gearshift cover of Ross's vehicle that hadn't been accounted for, and the broken beer bottles in the foyer. The ceramic fragment with the sliver of glass and enquiries at the bottle shops also suggested the bottles were not broken in the afternoon, as Ross claimed.

Finally, Peter came back to the ring of blood on the partition. Peter again stated that police strongly believed this occurred from someone having placed a beer bottle in Judith's blood, then lifting the bottle and sitting it on the partition.

Ross responded with, 'It could have been me. I'm not saying it was me. I found out things here that you've completely shocked me with.'

Alex Pollock took the opportunity to offer Ross a suggestion. Could Ross have retrieved the bottles of beer from his fridge? Ross had a beer fridge in his garage. Ross didn't accept this scenario. He didn't have any beer at his home that day, and that was why he bought the two bottles after leaving the Tavern.

Going over pictures of Judith's body, Peter brought Ross's attention to the cuts and bruising on his wife's right forearm. Shards of beer glass had dispersed around the floor next to her right arm and some fine shards had stuck to Judith's skin. Peter asked Ross what he would think of a suggestion that a beer bottle had been broken against Judith's arm. Ross agreed it was a possibility.

Peter admitted that he had spoken to a lot of people who supported Ross's statement that he loved Judith. He didn't believe otherwise. Peter also believed that something happened on the Friday morning to set Ross off. It might have been an argument over the finances and the fact that Judith and Ross were struggling a bit to make ends meet.

When Peter mentioned the state of Ross's finances, Ross took great exception. He didn't accept there were any financial problems in the family. They owned everything; all they had to pay for was rent and 'tucker'.

To get a better picture of Ross and Judith's finances, Alex Pollock jumped in and asked Ross to take him through all the dealings from just before they left Singleton, including the sale of the Gardener Circuit house, paying off debts that included paying out his and Judith's vehicle loans, the redundancy package, the move to Anna Bay, and the sale of the Tanilba Bay home. Alex also had Ross account for every dollar he and Judith received.

Ross admitted that Judith had looked after the accounts. He offered no explanation for why the bulk of their money was in a fixed term deposit in Judith's name only. Because Ross wasn't working he had applied for social security, but due to the interest being earned on the money in the fixed term account, he received a fortnightly cheque of only $40.00. Two days before the murder on 31 May, Ross contacted his bank to get a replacement credit card. His existing card had 'had the prawn'; it was split and curved and so he had thrown it into the bin. When he spoke to the bank he made the comment that he was expecting $200 to be placed into his savings account. When asked where the money was coming from, he told the detectives that it was owed to him by a 'friend'.

Alex asked Ross if, at the time he called the bank, he was aware his account was overdrawn.

Ross claimed he wasn't. He had accessed the account a 'couple of times' to see if the money he was expecting had come through, but wasn't aware of it being overdrawn.

When Peter asked about why Ross phoned the bank to change the fixed deposit back into both their names, Ross had a simple answer: 'Just to enquire, was it possible [sic]. That's all it was, it was just an outright enquiry and he said to me, yes, if Jude wants to come in and I never worried about it.'

Ross was reminded that during the conversation with the bank about the term deposit account he told the manager he wanted to make the change 'because there's some funny business going on, if you know what I mean'. What, exactly, did he mean?

Ross didn't give a straight answer. He said, 'Well, everyone has an off day, like I'm, you know yourself, like your marriage don't run perfect three hundred and sixty-five days a year, I may have had a bit of a bee in me bonnet'.

Despite saying they never argued, Ross admitted his reference to 'funny business' may have been because Judith had come home late 'with the shits' and they had had 'a couple of words'. Ross quickly clarified the issue by stating again, 'We didn't fight or nothing like that'.

Alex picked up on this point. Was Ross saying he and Judith had an argument on 1 June?

Ross denied it. He did, however, concede that he and Judith would have the occasional words, mostly at Judith's instigation. The arguments would be about Judith's annoyance at Ross for having been at the pub during the day.

Was it possible, Alex asked, that Ross had similar words with Judith on the Friday morning?

'No. I kissed my wife Friday morning before I left, I'm pretty sure I did, I loved my wife,' came Ross's answer. He took a moment to think, then it struck him. 'I get the feeling here that you guys are trying to tell me that I murdered my wife.'

Alex calmly explained that he and Peter were only acting on information that had been gathered by the investigation, and they need to ask Ross questions because the information they had pointed to him as being the main suspect.

Instead of protesting his innocence, Ross kept saying he was 'in shock' concerning the evidence that showed he hadn't purchased the two bottles of beer. 'I was a hundred percent sure I bought them [bottles of beer] there [the Tavern bottle shop] and I still say that today.'

Alex picked up on Ross's insistence that he loved his wife and that he and Judith had a wonderful relationship. Changing tack, he asked if that were so, why hadn't Ross ever called Peter, Graeme Parker, or any other detective on the taskforce to find out how the investigation into his wife's murder was progressing? Surely Ross would want to know Judith's murder hadn't been forgotten? Ross agreed. He did care, but he also didn't want to 'bother' Peter or any of the other detectives. Ross figured if they had information they would have called him.

Alex was a little taken aback. He felt as if Ross was treating the investigation into his wife's murder as though it were just an inquiry into a stolen car. When asked if he thought it strange he hadn't contacted the investigation, Ross simply answered, 'No, I don't'.

It was then brought up that Ross had not shown any grief in relation to Judith's death, rather, he displayed anger and rage. Alex had viewed the videotapes of the Friday evening interview and the walk-through, but hadn't seen any reaction that could have been described as grief-stricken. He asked Ross to explain why he hadn't shown any emotion.

'I'm a person who holds it inside them, sir,' Ross replied. He added that he never showed emotion, just like his father, though privately he had cried for hours.

Alex reminded Ross that Judith hadn't just died, she was brutally murdered. To the surprise of Alex and Peter, Ross said he 'didn't know it was a brutal murder'. How could Ross not be aware of how Judith had died? Having discovered his wife he would have surely concluded it was a brutal attack?

Ross said he didn't know because no one told him. He had never asked how his wife had died. No police officer, any member of the investigation team, ever mentioned to him that Judith had been brutally murdered. On the afternoon of the murder Ross said he was in shock when he discovered his wife. He remembered there being a lot of blood, but because police wouldn't allow him to go back in he couldn't say how his wife had died.

Alex moved on to the issue of what clothing Ross had been wearing that day. Ross immediately said he had been wearing blue jeans and a jacket, the green bomber jacket police had taken on the Friday evening. According to Joel, his father had been wearing a grey flannel shirt and black tracksuit pants. Alex showed Ross photos of the laundry and the clothes basket with the damp grey flannel shirt. Ross said he owned two grey flannels, and that they were usually washed separately 'because the amount of stuff that comes off them when you wash it, it sticks to everything'.

Peter interjected, wanting to clarify with Ross which grey flannel they were talking about. The flannel as observed by police at the scene had a Howick open cut mines insignia. Ross denied either flannel had an emblem on it. The only apparel he had with the logo was his green bomber jacket. Ross eventually agreed that the grey flannel did have small red writing on it, attributed to the mining company.

The other point Peter wanted to know was why the clothes, the grey flannel and Judith's nightgown, were placed in the second basket. Ross agreed the basket that had the damp clothing was normally the dirty clothes basket. Why then, if they had been washed, were the two pieces of apparel not included with the other washing in the basket on top of the washing machine? Why have them separate?

'I don't know, Peter, because I don't, I didn't even know that was there and my grey flannel, ah, sometimes I get it out of there and wear it again if it was cold and I was going outside for a smoke, because we never smoke inside, um, I had my green Howick jacket on, it's grey, it's not grey, it's green, it's got a Howick emblem there.'

Ross did do the washing at times, but said he didn't do any washing that morning. He couldn't explain how or why his flannel and Judith's nightie ended up in the basket, but he was adamant he only wore his green bomber jacket on the Friday.

Alex decided to present Ross with a scenario of what happened on the Friday morning. He put it to Ross that he and Judith had an argument. It was an intense argument, and Ross struck out at her and killed her, and then left the house with the dog. Then, when Ross arrived back home that afternoon he staged his shock at discovering his wife by purposely smashing the bottles of beer and dropping his keys, then running out and calling for help.

Ross denied ever hitting Judith. He never had and he never would. He didn't stage the dropping of the beer bottles or his keys. He couldn't remember exactly how it all happened, but as soon as he saw Judith's body he lost his grip on the bottles. Again, despite the surveillance tapes and cash register receipts, Ross was insistent he bought the two long-necked bottles of Toohey's New from the Anna Bay Tavern Bottle Shop.

Alex raised another point. Was it usual for Ross to leave before Judith went to work if all he was doing was taking the dog for a run? After all, if Ross's recollection of the time he departed was correct, he just had to wait ten to fifteen minutes before he and Judith could have left together. So why not wait?

The question was not properly addressed by Ross. Instead, he claimed he didn't have a set routine. Sometimes he would take all three boys to school and then go on and walk the dog, or go fishing, it all depended on his mood. Regardless of how Peter tried to get Ross to answer Alex's proposition, Ross just mumbled and re-enacted his farewell: 'Love you, darl … no, I love you, darl … I'm going.' It was as though Ross felt that was a sufficient response.

Speaking with Ross's three boys, Peter knew that Ross was expected to pick up Riley after school on the Friday and then drive Joel and a another boy to the southern Newcastle suburb of Valentine, about a one-hour drive from Anna Bay, for rugby league practice. It was a regular excursion for Ross. The only exception to the routine, Riley had told police, was when his father had a job interview or an appointment with Centrelink.

Ross couldn't say whether he had an interview or needed to be at Centrelink. He normally visited Centrelink's job centre on a Wednesday. He also refuted having to pick Riley up and taking Joel to Valentine. He had had a 'belly full of beer' and was certain another parent was transporting the boys.

This excuse of Ross's was counted when Peter told him he had mentioned to one person at the Tavern that he had to take the kids to practice, and he even called other parents the day before to confirm details.

Peter put it to Ross that, given that he had been

drinking well over the legal limit that day, why would he even consider picking up Joel and putting himself and his son at such great risk on the drive? Ross claimed he would never have driven with the amount of alcohol he had in his system. Again suggesting he didn't have to take Joel to practice, he said he would have called one of the other parents and had them take the boys. Even so, when asked if he had ever done this, Ross admitted he hadn't, and that his boys came before him. If he'd known he was going to drive to Valentine, he would only have had a couple of beers in the morning, if that. He was a very responsible parent.

On the topic of responsibility, Alex then suggested that as Ross was a responsible parent and loved his children, he would not have wanted his boys to see their mother lying bloodied and beaten in the foyer. Perhaps that was the reason Ross went straight home from the Tavern and not collected Riley on the way, arriving before the other two boys and saving them from witnessing the horror he knew was there?

'I never killed my wife,' Ross answered. 'I loved her, mate, and I never. I'm telling you, no, I'm sorry, I didn't kill my wife.'

Going back to the crime scene, Alex noted that only the main bedroom had been ransacked, while the rest of the house remained untouched. Coincidentally, Ross's shoeprints led from Judith's body to the bedroom and no other room in the house. Alex then suggested that it was Ross who pulled all the clothing from the drawers and wardrobe, and spilled out the contents of the jewellery box, either after the murder or when he returned in the afternoon.

Naturally, Ross denied this allegation.

Peter explained that in his experience, and the experience of other police who had viewed the scene, the ransacking of the bedroom appeared staged. The laying of the clothing and spreading of the jewellery was all too careful and ordered for a break and enter. Peter also reminded Ross that, during the walk-through, he claimed some items, other than Judith's purse, bag, and keys, were missing: football boots belonging to the boys and one of Judith's chains.

Ross admitted he had found the football boots and Judith's chain. There was nothing missing from the jewellery box. It was all accounted for.

Peter was perplexed. 'So among all that jewellery, someone has gone through all that jewellery, put it aside and they've taken nothing, none of that jewellery has been taken, they've just shuffled it?'

Judith apparently didn't own expensive jewellery, according to Ross. That didn't sit right with Peter. He couldn't believe that a thief would know or care if the jewellery was expensive or not. In his experience, thieves take whatever they can get their hands on and worry about its value later.

Ross suggested there might be items still missing, as he wasn't altogether familiar with everything Judith owned. Even so, as Peter pointed out, the television, video, and none of the other major electrical items were ever touched. Electrical appliances are normally the main target of those committing break and enters. All Ross could say was he still had them.

It was almost two and a half hours from when the interview had begun. Peter decided to wrap it up. He thought he'd take the opportunity to be frank with Ross and tell him how he believed Judith's death had come about. With little interruption, Ross sat listening to what Peter had to say.

Peter accepted that Ross did love Judith. People police had spoken to verified that Ross and Judith seemed to have had a loving relationship. Although Ross claimed he and Judith never argued, police had learned the couple did have disagreements. The main reason for them was Ross's drinking and gambling. On one occasion while at Singleton, the police had learned, Judith locked Ross out on the pergola as punishment for losing money on the pokies.

Given this history, Peter figured that Ross and Judith had had an argument on the Friday morning, most likely over finances. Ross wasn't working and Judith was worried about being able to meet the rent and buy food without dipping into their savings. Ross had tried to secure a job, but was finding it difficult. On the Friday morning, Peter believed, Judith made a comment, probably out of frustration, about Ross spending the day down at the Tavern while she had to go to work. Ross had admitted in earlier interviews that he had a short temper, and, what with the pressures of being unemployed, Ross snapped back, and before he knew it Judith was on the ground. She was dead.

After Ross's rage cleared, he realised what he had done. He panicked. He didn't know what to do, so he took his dog and the statue, and spent the day in the Tavern trying to clear his head. Thinking of his boys, not wanting to leave them, Ross returned home and staged the break and enter. It was all he could think of doing to keep what was left of his family together.

Having explained this scenario, Peter tried to coax Ross into telling him what really happened. He appealed to Ross's love for his boys, saying that it was better for them to hear it from their father than later after an extracted court process. With all the evidence presented, Ross was the only possible suspect and Peter hoped he would make it easy on himself and his sons. Peter even read some of Dr Diamond's report, which stated that the murder was committed 'in a moment of intensity and rage', supporting Peter's theory that Ross had just exploded without thinking.

After Peter had spoken for some time, Ross asked if he could speak.

'I was a hundred percent sure I bought my beer at the pub at Anna Bay and to this day I know you've gone down there and everything, mate, you can go and ask [Joe] again, I'd like you to. I am positive I bought my beer there and as long as I'm sitting here, while I'm alive and on my father's dying oath I never killed my wife.'

Peter and Alex went back over some of the evidence, highlighting all the inconsistencies in his story and what they had found to be fact, but Ross never changed his answers; he preferred to ignore the evidence being presented to him and to stick with his version of events. However hard they tried, Peter and Alex failed to break down Ross's resolve.

By the end of the interview Ross was in no doubt that Peter suspected him, and him alone, of having murdered Judith. As Ross hadn't confessed, Peter now had to rely on his contingency plan. At Maitland Police Station, unbeknown to Ross, Murray had been fitted with a wire. Police explained to Murray that they wanted him to engage Ross in conversation while on their trip back to Singleton. It was hoped Ross might react to the interview and let slip something incriminating when talking to his friend.

On the drive back to Singleton that afternoon, Ross appeared to speak openly with Murray about most of what was discussed during the interview. As in the interview, Ross explained away the allegations. He didn't say anything contrary to what he had told Peter Fox and Alex Pollock.

The listening device left Peter scratching his head. His hope that Ross might slip up and say something that would incriminate him was quashed. Nevertheless, the fact that Ross was obviously very careful with what he had to say only added to Peter's initial suspicions. Did Ross suspect—or know—that police would use a listening device?

Whatever reason Ross had for not elaborating on his interrogation, the fact was that installing the listening device had not worked. Normally, as a matter of course, typewritten transcripts are made of all tapes. On this occasion, the tapes contained nothing that would assist Peter judicially, so no transcript was ever ordered.

Still, Peter wasn't giving up. Peter believed Ross was keeping his involvement in the murder close to his chest. He didn't appear to have confided in anyone, and was obviously attempting to convince friends and relatives of his innocence. Peter knew he wouldn't be getting any late confession out of his suspect, so he had to rely on the physical evidence if he was to build a strong circumstantial case.

Even though Peter's efforts at trying to get more evidence against Ross by using a listening device hadn't progressed the investigation, Peter still couldn't let the matter rest. He knew there was always something else. Sometimes it could be something very small, a minor detail that, because of the frenetic nature of investigations at the start, might have been overlooked.

In between dealing with other matters at work and getting some DIY done at his home, Peter put himself in Judith's place. He kept thinking about what Judith would have done to protect herself, or at least fight off the assault. Could the killer have left some minute trace of evidence yet to be discovered? If so, where would or could it be found?

While Judith's defence wounds were minimal—only because the attack was sudden and she was put into a defenceless position from the beginning—Peter couldn't stop thinking about the watch. The clear plastic cover had broken away, exposing the face, which obviously received the blow that bent one of the hands. He couldn't explain why, but he felt it was worth taking a closer look at the watch face.

After mulling the idea over on a weekend, Peter returned to work on the Monday and went straight to Peter Muscio's office. As they shared a coffee, Peter Fox explained his theory that maybe, just maybe, something on the face of the watch could have been trace evidence from the murderer. Peter Muscio was less than convinced. He had been over the watch numerous times and not found anything. In fact, he commented that the detective sergeant 'had been watching too many police shows on telly'.

Peter Fox was insistent. He asked the crime scene examiner to indulge him. After all, it would only take a few minutes to check. The two men went to the evidence room and signed out the watch, which was still in the original bag from the afternoon of the murder. They went back to the crime scene offices where Peter Muscio brought out a high-powered microscope.

Placing the watch under the microscope, Peter Muscio began to grin, and with a tinge of excitement in his voice turned to the detective and said, 'Foxy, you are a dead-set arse!'

Peter Fox lit up. He couldn't believe it. Could whatever Peter Muscio found be linked back to Judith's killer? Fox couldn't wait to know the result. He grabbed the scope to see for himself.

Peter Muscio had found very fine lengths of fabric caught on the centre pin of the watch. They could have got there only after the clear cover had been knocked away. This meant Judith's watch had come into contact with an article of clothing. Both men hoped the fibres came from clothing worn by the killer.

Peter Fox thought about what to do next. They had clothing from Ross and Judith, as well as carpet samples; they could use these to compare the composition of the fibres. As hopeful as they were, there was an even chance that the fibres might have come from Judith's clothes as much as easily as from those of her killer, or even from the carpet. Other than the clothing police had taken from Ross on the Friday evening, there was still the grey flannel shirt his son Joel mentioned in his statement. Would the fibre match the grey shirt?

Before they could even begin to match the fibre, they needed it to be identified. The two men turned to Professor Claude Roux, director of the University of Technology Sydney's Centre for Forensic Science. Professor Roux is regarded as one of the foremost experts in textile fibres. He has worked with law enforcement agencies across Australia in examining textiles in criminal cases. Also, the centre held state-of-the-art equipment to identify the items. Peter Fox personally drove down to Sydney and delivered the watch with the fibres intact for Professor Roux to study. It would be some time before the results came back.

With this new evidence Peter decided he would speak with Ross's two older boys, Joel and Riley. Peter planned to speak to both boys without Ross's knowledge. The reason for this move was obvious: as their father was the prime suspect, Peter wanted them to feel they could speak candidly. The rationale for the interviews was to confirm with Joel his original statement in which he told detectives his father had been wearing a grey flannel shirt and black tracksuit pants on the Friday morning. Likewise, Peter hoped Riley might provide some additional information on his father, as Ross had driven his eldest son to school that day.

The interviews were planned for 27 November. Peter Fox, along with other detectives from Maitland, attended Joel's school. After speaking with the principal, Joel was taken from the school by police to take part in an electronic record of interview. In normal circumstances, as Joel was a minor Ross would have been required to sit in on the interview, being Joel's father. On this occasion, not wanting Ross to be present, Peter organised for a welfare worker from the Department of Community Services to be there to look out for Joel's wellbeing and to ensure his rights.

In the more formal setting of an interview, Joel gave Peter more details than he had in his previous statement. The boy said his father hadn't returned home from taking Riley to school. Ross had Floyd with him; he usually went straight from dropping Riley to the beach to exercise the dog. Joel also remembered seeing his father drive past his school on the morning of the murder. Joel had entered the school grounds when he noticed the four-wheel-drive. Ross drove past the school and turned right into The Esplanade in the direction of the family home.

Joel confirmed again that he was positive his father had not been wearing the clothing he was dressed in on the Friday evening at Nelson Bay Police Station, but had worn a grey flannel shirt with an emblem of the Howick Mining Company Ross had previously worked for in Singleton, very similar to the shirt police had noticed was left damp in the washing basket. Along with the shirt, Joel believed his father had been wearing a pair of black tracksuit trousers.

The only discrepancy between Joel's interview and the statement he'd given police earlier was whether Ross had returned home before he and his younger brother left for school. In his statement he said he had kissed both parents goodbye, yet in his interview he said he was sure Ross hadn't retuned home. The next time Joel spotted his father was near 9.00, when Ross drove past the school heading towards Clonmeen Circuit. Ross driving past the school was consistent in Joel's statement and his interview.

In Ross's interviews, he had told police each time that he left the Clonmeen Street address soon after Joel and Gene, just before or at nine, and had gone straight to the beach to exercise the dog, picking up fuel at a service station on the way.

Joel's version of events led Peter to again wonder about a possible scenario he had thought of earlier. It might have been that, as both boys stated, Ross had planned to go straight to the beach after dropping Riley at school because he had taken Floyd with him. This would now fit if Joel was correct and Ross had not returned home. If so, Ross, as he had said, was now running low on fuel and stopped at the service station to purchase $10 or $15 worth of diesel. With only $30 or $40 in his pocket, Peter then surmised that Ross would have realised he had little money left to spend at the Tavern. This, then, might have been reason enough for Ross to return home in the hope that he could borrow some money from Judith. He would have had to get back home before 9.15 to catch Judith before she left for work. As Judith felt finances were tight, Ross asking for money to spend at the local pub could have been enough to start an argument.

While Joel's recollection about seeing his father drive past the school fitted Peter's scenario, placing Ross back at the house after 9.00, and it matched the statement made by the neighbour who had seen his vehicle, it still wasn't concrete enough. There was no way of knowing, even if Ross admitted to driving past Joel's school, that he had gone home. And, because of earlier enquiries, Peter knew he'd never be able to say when, even if, Ross bought the diesel from the service station.

Once Joel's interview was completed, police drove the boy home. Ross wasn't there, so Joel was then taken to a family friend's house. Joel would make his own way back to Wilcox Avenue once he was sure his father was at home.

Peter Fox then picked up Riley and formally interviewed him in the presence of the welfare worker. Riley didn't give police anything more than they already knew.

When Riley's interview was concluded, Peter Fox and the other detectives drove him home. Ross met them at the front door. Peter looked past Ross, who was standing in the doorway, and saw Joel sitting in the living room. Ross appeared quizzical at finding Peter with his eldest son. Peter answered Ross's curiosity with, 'We've had both Riley and Joel down to the station. We spoke to them about their mum's murder. Joel has probably told you about it, has he?'

Ross appeared genuinely surprised at the news and turned to Joel, saying, 'No, he hasn't'.

Within half an hour of delivering Riley home, the police officers observed Ross and Joel leave the premises and get into the four-wheel-drive. They drove off and neither returned for a considerable time that afternoon. There was no way for police to know what Ross and his son discussed while they were away from home.

It was around this time that Peter learned of Ross's drug habit. Ross was using illicit drugs and was on the methadone program. Methadone is a synthetic drug prescribed to addicts to help reduce and/or eliminate their dependency on heroin. It relieves the narcotic cravings, suppresses the side effects associated with withdrawal through abstinence, and blocks the euphoric feelings induced by heroin.

Police had also observed Ross making several visits to the home of the known drug dealer. What caught Peter's attention wasn't the association as much as it was the drug dealer in question. The dealer had recently been released from gaol after an intensive investigation several years earlier that led to his arrest and conviction. Peter Fox led that investigation, during which he employed a listening device to collect evidence against the dealer. The DPP then used the tapes, which caught the dealer talking about drugs and supplying users, during the trial.

There was no way to know for sure, but Peter was of the opinion that the dealer might have mentioned the use of listening devices to Ross. After all, if Ross had spoken to the dealer about Judith's murder and Peter Fox's name was brought up, particularly as Ross knew he was a prime suspect, it is likely the dealer would mention about how he was caught by covert surveillance. This could then have explained why Ross appeared cautious in talking about the murder to Murray, just in case anything slipped out that could be incriminating.

Soon after speaking with the two boys, Ross's solicitor contacted Peter and explained that he had advised his client not to take part in any further interviews. This call wasn't unexpected. Peter felt he wouldn't gain much by talking to Ross again, anyway. Having got to know Ross, Peter believed he only went through the first two interviews—on the night of the murder and the subsequent walk-through—to help convince family, friends, and police that he hadn't committed the crime. Ross's ploy had not been successful. As Peter was learning, more and more friends suspected Ross of murdering Judith, so for Ross, there was probably no point in continuing to be helpful to police. Peter knew that now he would have to rely on the physical evidence and hope there would be more to come.

Based on the information from Joel regarding the grey flannel shirt, Peter organised for a warrant to search the Wilcox Avenue address. If Ross had killed Judith while wearing the shirt, Peter expected blood would be detected. No matter how well fabric is washed the bloodstain remains, although it is not obvious to the naked eye. Chemicals have to be used to highlight the stain. But if, as Peter suspected, Ross had quickly washed the shirt the morning of the murder, the blood would be contaminated, making it difficult to match with Judith's type. Even so, the pattern of the staining, the amount of blood present, and the fact that police would find blood all went towards Peter's mounting circumstantial case against Ross. As well, there could be a chance the fibres found on Judith's watch could be matched to the shirt.

So, on 6 December, Peter attended the Brown home with other detectives. They executed the warrant as Ross looked on, collecting two grey flannel shirts and pair of blue tracksuit pants. Despite Ross not wanting to assist police with any further interviews, he was still courteous and friendly towards the detectives. But the two shirts and the tracksuit pants were not the type described by Joel and witnessed by the police on the afternoon of the murder. There was no open cut mining insignia on either shirt. Peter asked Ross where the grey flannel shirt was that had the logo. Ross denied ever having such a shirt. The two grey flannels Peter held were all he ever owned. There was nothing Peter could do. A thorough search of the house didn't reveal the shirt hidden anywhere. Peter packed the shirts and pants in an evidence bag and took them back to Maitland.

Peter Muscio studied the clothing from Wilcox Avenue, but there was no blood present on any of the items. There was nothing that Peter could find to link the shirts and pants to the crime scene. No fine glass fragments and no cement dust or particles either: the clothing was clean. If Ross had worn the grey flannel shirt with the Howick Open Cut Mine insignia on the day of the murder, he had obviously disposed of it some time after.

Peter received some more news. Professor Roux had examined the fibres and made his assessment. He called Peter with the results. Unfortunately for Peter, the fibres were common cotton and found in most apparel; they were not unique in any way. So common were the fibres that there would be no way of saying exactly which item of clothing they had come from. There would be no way of linking them to either Ross's or Judith's clothes. They could have come from a pair of jeans, a shirt, a casual top, slacks—anything and anyone. The fibres were also common white, so they couldn't even be matched by colour to any of the clothing, but that didn't mean they hadn't come from any of the apparel worn by Ross or Judith.

In Peter's words the news 'knocked the wind out of me. We had such high hopes ... We really thought we'd had it. We gave it a go, but it just didn't pan out. We went back to the drawing board.'

Still, Peter refused to give up. He sat with Peter Muscio and other colleagues and tossed around ideas and thoughts on the other physical evidence. Was there anything they had missed? Was it worth going back over some of the items?

~

With school holidays having started, and Christmas and New Year approaching fast, Peter Fox decided to renew his appeal for the missing statue. He spoke with Frances O'Shea from Sydney's *Daily Telegraph*, telling her, for the first time, that Judith most likely knew her killer. Peter had never before suggested whether Judith had died at the hands of someone familiar to her or whether it was a botched break-in.

'There were no signs of forced entry and indications are that Mrs Brown's killer might have been known to her,' Peter told the journalist.

Naturally, if the perpetrator was someone Judith knew, Frances O'Shea asked about her husband, knowing he had been interviewed on at least two occasions. Peter wouldn't let himself be drawn into making any accusations; he simply said that the family had been assisting him with the investigation.

As holiday makers began arriving in the area for the sun, surf, and sand, Peter again hoped someone might come across the statue, Judith's handbag, her purse and keys. He explained to Frances O'Shea that, 'with the annual influx of tourists in the Anna Bay area, it is possible someone may find these items in bushland … It is vital if they find anything relevant to this inquiry that they contact police immediately.'

By the end of 2000 and the start of 2001, no one had come across the swagman statue or any of Judith's belongings. Peter had exhausted every lead he had. There was little more he could do. For the first time during the investigation, Peter Fox began to lose hope.

Peter reviewed what evidence he had. He could prove Ross had not bought buy two long-necked bottles of Toohey's New on the afternoon of the murder. The swagman statue, used by the Brown family as a doorstop, was the murder weapon. The broken piece of ceramic with the sliver of glass stuck to it under the blood suggested that a beer bottle had been smashed at the time Judith was assaulted. Forensic psychologist Michael Diamond's assessment of the crime scene, the interview tapes and transcripts showed Ross's behaviour to be suspicious and inconsistent with 'someone who may be grief-stricken or overwhelmed'. Dr Diamond also believed Judith's attacker was 'someone with who she felt comfortable and familiar'. Then there was Joel's evidence of the grey flannel shirt with the logo and the fact that he saw his father driving past his school towards Clonmeen Circuit near nine o'clock on the Friday morning. As well, Danni, a neighbour, who saw Ross's vehicle parked in the driveway at around 9.10, had a good reason to be aware of the time. There was also Ross's excessive drinking on the day of the murder, his failure to keep to his routine of collecting his eldest son in the afternoon, and failing to drive Joel and another boy to footy training as he had arranged, all of which was out of character.

As a motive, Peter had Ross's erratic spending habit, having exhausted all of his and Judith's savings, the call to the bank the day before the murder to get access to the fixed term account that was in Judith's name, and selling Judith's car and the continued spending spree after moving back to Singleton.

Peter had some physical evidence and a lot of suspicion, but he realised all this still wasn't enough to arrest and hold Ross for murder. He knew he had the right suspect, but he couldn't prove it beyond a reasonable doubt. In New South Wales a jury must come to a unanimous verdict if finding the defendant guilty. It takes only one juror to have doubt for a mistrial to occur. Peter didn't want to take the risk. He just didn't have enough evidence, even for a circumstantial case.

The only option open to Peter was to prepare a brief for the coroner. A coronial inquest would, as Peter had, review the evidence and then make a finding as to the cause of death and who might be responsible. An inquest can sometimes be useful for police in generating publicity and gathering more evidence. Also, the coroner might actually name Ross as a person of interest in the death of his wife, without requiring the same level of evidence against him that would be needed for a trial.

The findings of a coronial inquest could give Judith's family and friends some closure, if only to explain how Judith died and who was most likely responsible. By pointing the finger at Ross, it might also bring out witnesses, as yet unknown to police, who had information that could add to the prosecution case.

Chapter 9

BREAKING THE SILENCE

During January and February 2001 Peter Fox was losing all hope of ever finding the swagman statue, Judith's bag, her purse and keys. If anyone had come across any of the items they probably didn't realise their relevance and just saw them as being discarded junk. As the summer holidays came to end, children went back to school, parents began work, and life returned to normal. The tourists left Anna Bay and the small seaside hamlet went back to being its quiet, tranquil self. For the residents of the area, and for Peter, the murder of Judith Brown wasn't far from their minds, especially as justice had yet to be done.

Peter's investigation appeared to have run its course; he was filled with frustration. It wasn't a unique situation the seasoned detective found himself in: he'd had cases before where he knew who had committed the crime, had the physical evidence to support his theory on how the murder had happened, yet didn't have enough evidence to take the matter before a jury. Even Peter's colleagues were uncertain if the case would ever result in a conviction.

Although the evidence Peter had obtained proved inconsistencies in Ross's story, there was no knowing how the evidence would stand up under cross-examination from the defence counsel, and a prosecutor must convince a jury of a person's guilt beyond a reasonable doubt. Based on the evidence they had collected, Peter and the taskforce were certainly convinced of Ross's guilt, but an experienced defence team could find alternative reasons for some of the evidence and raise enough doubt to bring about a mistrial or even an acquittal.

As Peter became caught up in other matters requiring his attention, he also began putting together a brief on the murder of Judith Brown for a coronial inquiry. In these first few months of the year Peter still hadn't heard a whisper from Ross. Even after pointing out his apparent lack of concern for the investigation into his wife's death, it obviously made no impression on Ross, who remained conspicuous by his absence. Peter did, however, receive calls from Judith's friends, all of whom enquired how the investigation was progressing and shared their growing suspicions regarding Ross. For all their good intentions, none of Judith's friends had any information that could help Peter.

In March 2001, just as Peter was about to sign off on Judith's case and leave it in the hands of the coroner, he received a call from two people in Singleton who knew Judith and Ross well. Henry and Phyllis (not their real names), were close to Judith and had been helping Ross and the boys settle back into the community since Judith's murder. Like other friends, Henry and Phyllis also had their suspicions about Ross's involvement. They had not spoken with police earlier because they had little to say. Now, having had discussions with Ross prior to and after the murder, Henry and Phyllis had become concerned about the content of these discussions and decided to contact Peter.

Peter travelled to Singleton to meet with Henry and Phyllis. Phyllis in particular made it known she was reluctant to make a formal statement. They just wanted to get things off their chest. This isn't unusual: people often want to tell police what they know but do not wish to be involved in giving evidence at a trial.

Sitting in the lounge room, Peter was unsure about Phyllis and Henry. He didn't know if they had anything to offer the investigation, or whether, as can happen, they were trying to get information from Peter to pass on to Ross. Phyllis admitted she didn't want to believe Ross was involved in his wife's murder, but there were certain things that bothered her, things that led her to come to the opinion that Ross had killed Judith.

Peter played it defensively. He didn't give anything away and allowed Phyllis and Henry to do all the talking.

They told Peter they had known Judith and Ross for some years, and corroborated other information given by friends about the Browns' relationship while living in Singleton. Some time in May 2000, Ross travelled back to the Upper Hunter mining town and visited Henry and Phyllis. While Henry and Ross were having a smoke and talking out the back, Ross decided to have a heart to heart. He disclosed that Judith was 'having an affair with a younger man'. He didn't volunteer a name for Judith's lover. He also confided that 'There is a large amount of money missing out of the account ... she has got all the money tied up in her name'.

After Ross left, Henry confided what had been said to Phyllis. It surprised them. They had thought Ross and Judith's relationship was solid, particularly as they had just moved to Anna Bay and seemed to be starting their lives afresh. The couple were shocked by the news and took pity on Ross and the three boys.

On Wednesday 31 May 2000, two days before the murder, Henry received a call from Ross. He wanted to borrow $250 to fill his four-wheel-drive with fuel to take Joel to rugby league practice on the Friday afternoon. Henry couldn't lend Ross the money; he didn't have any spare cash. Ross called Henry another couple of times on that day, but Henry was unavailable so Phyllis took the calls. Phyllis took the opportunity to inform Ross that Henry had told her about the affair and the missing money. Worried that the affair would be affecting the family, Phyllis enquired about the welfare of the three boys. Ross said they were 'holding up okay'. When Phyllis asked about Judith, Ross gave an ominous reply, 'I'll give her to Friday'.

Speaking to Peter, Phyllis said she didn't realise until later that Friday was the day Judith had been murdered. Ross's words had been haunting her ever since. Some time after Judith's death, she spoke to Murray, who had accompanied Ross to each of his interviews with police, and told him about Ross's allegation that Judith was having an affair and that was money missing. Murray was confused. Ross had never mentioned this to police and police weren't looking at Judith as having an affair. Phyllis's doubts grew.

Two days after Judith's murder, on Sunday 4 June, Henry accompanied Ross to watch the rugby league match Riley was playing in. At the game, Ross borrowed $100 from Henry. Henry and Phyllis assisted Ross with the move from Anna Bay to the Wilcox Avenue address.

Before contacting Peter, Henry and Phyllis urged Ross to phone Task Force Saltpond and pass on the information about Judith's affair and the missing money. Ross shrugged them off.

Peter was curious about one thing. As Henry and Phyllis helped Ross move all his furnishings and belongings from Clonmeen Circuit to Anna Bay, did they recall taking two washing baskets from the laundry? If so, did they remember the contents of one of the baskets?

As Peter had hoped, Henry and Phyllis both remembered the laundry baskets and described a grey flannel shirt they—and police—had seen in one of the baskets: it was a grey flannel shirt bearing the Howick Mining Company logo, the same flannel shirt police had been unable to locate at Ross's new house, and that he had denied owning.

What Henry and Phyllis had told Peter wasn't only revealing, but also supported other evidence he'd collected against Ross. Ross had made a call to his bank on Wednesday 31 May requesting a replacement credit card and telling them he was expecting $200 to be paid into his savings account. This was the same day the account had been depleted and become overdrawn. When Peter and Alex questioned Ross about the account, he replied that the $200 was coming from 'a friend' who owed him the money.

The reason Ross needed the money confirmed his intention to drive Joel and another boy to rugby league training on the Friday afternoon. Ross had told the detectives that he didn't think he had to drive to Valentine, and had only had 'a belly full of beer' because he was sure another parent was taking the boys. Henry's recollection of the phone call and other statements from parents and patrons at the Anna Bay Tavern all contradict Ross's story that he had not been planning to take Joel to practice.

In all the interviews and discussions Peter and his team had with Ross, he never once mentioned or even hinted that Judith had had an affair. Ross always presented himself and Judith as having a close and loving, almost perfect relationship. Admittedly, Ross might have felt embarrassed to have mentioned the affair, but considering Judith had been brutally murdered and police were looking at Ross as their prime suspect, it seemed unlikely to Peter or any of his colleagues that Ross wouldn't have come forward with this information. If Ross was innocent, why not say something about his suspicions, as Judith's lover might also be the killer?

If Ross were sincere in his belief about his wife's infidelity, could this have been a contributing factor to the argument that led to Judith's death? Did Ross kill Judith out of jealousy and for financial gain?

As Peter found out, Ross had not only told Henry and Phyllis of his suspicions regarding Judith's affair, but he also told other people around the Singleton area. Whether there was anything to substantiate the allegation or not, Peter would include this information in his brief and let the Director of Public Prosecutions decide if it could be used should Ross finally get to trial.

Personally, Peter didn't believe Judith had been having an affair. He felt Ross had used this story to gain sympathy from friends, maybe even to shift suspicion onto an anonymous secret lover. There was also no evidence that any money had gone missing from any of the accounts, other than the money Ross had withdrawn himself and the $80 000 he voluntarily put into the fixed term account that was in Judith's name.

To confirm whether calls were made to Henry and Phyllis on Wednesday 31 May, Peter checked with their phone records, which revealed that several reverse charge calls had been made to their number from the Brown residence on that day. The times corresponded with when Judith would have been at work and the boys were at school. The only possible person who could have made the calls was Ross Brown. This corroboration went towards showing Phyllis and Henry as being very credible witnesses.

As far as Ross's comment to Phyllis that he would give Judith 'till Friday', Peter knew this could mean almost anything. Although, given what had happened, it appeared incriminating, it could be explained in a number of ways. There was nothing specific to say that, two days before the murder, Ross had intended to kill his wife.

While Henry and Phyllis were initially reluctant to give a formal statement, Peter explained the importance of what they had told him. They might not have realised, but they had assisted Peter's investigation. After a short consideration, Henry and Phyllis agreed though this did not mean they would make a formal statement. They needed time to think it over. Even so the information they shared, injected new life into the hunt for Judith Brown's murderer.

With Henry and Phyllis having come forward, Peter began reviewing his evidence yet again. It was likely, given Henry and Phyllis' relationship with Ross, that they could gather further information that might assist the investigation. Ross might just slip up and say or intimate something that could prove to be incriminating. Henry and Phyllis had agreed to consider helping Peter if they could. They would keep in touch and let him know of any developments. How far Henry and Phyllis would go to help police would leave Peter more than astonished.

～

During the month of April Peter was kept busy when he was sent to the Police College at Goulburn, ironically, to attend the homicide course. With all of his experience of having worked on a number of homicides, and leading the inquiry into Judith Brown's murder, Peter was now hearing from other experienced detectives how to conduct a homicide investigation.

While at the college Peter sat through a presentation from retired Detective Superintendent Mike Hagan, who led the investigation into one of Australia's worst serial killers, John Wayne Glover the Granny Killer. The Granny Killer murdered six elderly women in Mosman, on Sydney's lower North Shore, between 1989 and 1990; police suspected him of an additional four murders. John Wayne Glover was eventually caught and sentenced to life imprisonment, never to be released. In 2005 he was found dead, hanging from a shower curtain in Lithgow Correctional Centre.

Mike Hagan has quite a reputation among Homicide detectives, all of whom hold him in great esteem as an investigator. What Hagan had to say that day was of particular interest to Peter. It had nothing to do with police procedure or any secrets about how to catch the bad guys, but rather about the type of person a homicide detective should be. When the retired superintendent began the investigation into the granny murders, a number of senior police officers contacted him to recommend staff, investigators, and analysts for his team. Mike Hagan admitted that the officers recommended to him were probably some of the very best, if not the best, at what they did, but he wasn't interested. Much to the surprise of senior police, he declined the offers. Hagan had his own criteria in selecting staff. He wanted police officers who were passionate about what they did.

This struck a chord with Peter, who had always wrestled with himself about how involved he became in a case, particularly during the investigation into the murder of Judith Brown. He wondered if he had allowed himself to become too involved. Should he be more removed, more clinical in his approach? Hearing Mike Hagan say that passion and commitment to a case were positive qualities made Peter feel better about his investigation. He didn't see himself as being obsessive, but rather passionate about solving the crime.

With regards to Judith's murder, Peter wanted to give the families closure, even though arresting Ross could mean dividing them. As much as Peter would have wanted everyone to be happy with the outcome, the reality was that the three boys could lose both parents. While the Homicide course was informative, what Peter most got out of it was knowing he was probably a better detective for having a passion to see justice served.

～

Henry and Phyllis made contact with Peter again in May and agreed to meet at Singleton Police Station. Most importantly, they had finally agreed to give a statement. When the couple walked into the station they were armed with more than just information. They proudly presented Peter with audio cassettes, having secretly taped conversations between themselves and

Ross. Peter's reaction was far from what Henry or Phyllis had expected: His face drained of blood and he treated the cassettes like a hot potato. He informed the couple that it was illegal to record anyone without their permission, and whatever was said, if it was considered valuable in evidence, could be argued inadmissible by the defence.

As helpful as Henry and Phyllis believed they were being, they may also have jeopardised any evidence they had collected by contravening the Listening Devices Act. Anyone being recorded must be informed, which is why call centres warn people and allow them the option of requesting that they not be taped. Before police can install listening devices they must first provide a good case for doing so and get the signature of a Supreme Court Judge. It was also an offence for Peter—or any police officer—to listen to the tapes, as they had been illegally recorded.

Peter immediately put the cassettes in an envelope and had Phyllis and Henry date and sign the seal. He wasn't taking any chances. But while it was illegal for Peter to listen to the tapes, it didn't mean he couldn't hear from Henry and Phyllis what had transpired.

Henry and Phyllis visited Ross at his home to confront him over rumours circulating the town. Ross apparently had been telling people that Henry was a drug supplier and he had been Henry's courier. Henry had the sort of solid build that would make it common for people to presume he was a tough guy, someone not to be messed about with, but he was no drug lord. It was thought by police that Ross's friendship with Henry was motivated because Ross wanted people to associate the two men as being friends. By this time, nearly a year after his wife's death, Ross was becoming more and more isolated as people began suspecting him of having had something to do with Judith's murder. Perhaps, by spreading the rumours, Ross felt people would think Henry would protect him should anyone have a go at him.

On hearing the rumours, Phyllis and Henry became angry. They couldn't believe Ross was saying such things and risking what friendship he had with the couple, not to mention Henry's safety and reputation by being labelled a drug baron. It was unbelievable. As his friends pressed him for answers, Ross became angry with them, not knowing that all the time he was being recorded by Phyllis who carried a microcassette concealed on her person. Ross didn't give anything away, avoiding direct answers.

In the end, the conversation became heated and, fuelled by her own suspicions, Phyllis wanted to know what Ross meant when he had told her 'going to give Judy to Friday'? Ross erupted and said he was giving Judith until Friday, and then he was 'going to leave her'. The situation had become too tense; the couple left.

Over the following weeks Ross made approaches to Henry and Phyllis to try to rekindle their friendship. On 3 May he invited them back over to his place. Phyllis took the opportunity to again record Ross using the concealed tape recorder. The atmosphere was more cordial this time around, and Ross seemed prepared to open up to his friends. He admitted to Henry and Phyllis that he had a drug problem, and was on the methadone program to try to curb his habit. As they discussed Judith having had an affair, Ross decided to tell them that he believed the name of the young man was Jack, though he knew little else about him. Pressed about the missing money, Ross conceded it was a banking error. He said $60 000 had gone from the account, but the bank eventually found it and readjusted the balance. There never was any money missing. The evening ended as it had begun, and for all Ross knew he still had Henry and Phyllis's support.

With regards to the investigation the tape recordings weren't a major development. They did commit Ross to his story that he believed Judith was having an affair, however unlikely it actually seemed. Peter wasn't sure how this information would assist the investigation, but it did confirm the earlier discussion Ross had had with Henry.

After a number of reports and speaking with Legal Services, Peter was advised he could legally have the tapes transcribed then sealed in an evidence bag, signed, and dated to protect the integrity of the recordings and prevent any subsequent allegation that the tapes might have been tampered with. It is possible that, while the recordings were illegal, in a trial where the severity of the offence is punishable by a life sentence, tapes can be ruled admissible by the trial judge, depending on their relevance against the defendant.

There was another legal loophole. Ross had been spreading lies about Henry being involved in the supply of drugs and it is considered lawful to secretly record another party for your own legal protection. Legal advice was that, whether she realised it or not, Phyllis might have had a legal right to secretly record her conversations with Ross. As it happened, most of the conversation between Ross, Henry, and Phyllis was about the spreading of the rumours. The transcripts were adopted into a statement and signed by Henry and Phyllis.

~

One year after the brutal murder of Judith Brown, the *Newcastle Herald* ran a two-page article focusing on the investigation. Journalist Jason Bartlett interviewed Detective Sergeant Peter Fox, telling his readers that 'Not a day goes by [when] the detective does not think about the mysterious murder of the mother of three, who lived an ordinary life in an ordinary community'.

Peter was happy about the publicity, hoping it might bring forward an as yet unknown witness or witnesses. Although Peter was sure his team was very thorough in getting statements from neighbours, friends, and relatives, there was still a chance they could have missed someone. It was possible that they did miss a vital witness, or there was a person out there who didn't want to become involved at the time and avoided police, or it could even be that a person was interviewed but had withheld information for reasons known only to them.

Peter told Jason Bartlett that 'Solving this murder is really important to us, it's really stayed in our minds … I work on this case every day … We've got two officers working full time on it even as we speak.'

The two officers Peter referred to were himself and Crime Scene Examiner Peter Muscio. The two Peters would meet almost daily, share a cup of coffee in the tea room or at their desks, and discuss all the evidence to date, trying to find anything they might have missed and what options were left for them to pursue.

Interestingly, Peter informed the journalist that the last people to see Judith alive on the Friday had been her two younger sons as they left for school. Peter was going on the information supplied by Joel in his record of interview, rather than what Ross had said. Ross had stated he was the last person to see his wife alive. Peter placed more credibility in Joel's recollections than Ross's.

The article also gave Peter the opportunity to make mention of the murder weapon, the swagman statue, and to ask people to keep an eye out for it, as well as Judith's brown handbag, leather purse and keys. Peter acknowledged that police had not stopped looking for them. It seems that Peter was still receiving calls from recycling yards and the public about statues they had found. He was encouraged that there was still great interest in the case.

Peter also mentioned that he was following some new lines of enquiry, which he could not elaborate on, and that he was re-interviewing witnesses. Peter was hopeful of getting a resolution to the case, though he stressed it might not be 'in the short term'.

Some areas of the media had been critical of the length of time the investigation had been taking. Peter was quick to respond to the criticism, saying, 'It's not that old a case ... We have worked on it continually since the beginning and not a week has gone by without enquiries being made ... If we can solve any case the following day, of course that's what we'd love to do, but the nature of murder cases is that some are more protracted than others.'

While Peter was being positive, he was also a realist. The anniversary of Judith's death was a sad occasion, and Peter felt particularly down. He still hadn't been able to give Judith's family the closure he wanted. Although Peter had re-interviewed witnesses and gone over all the physical evidence with Peter Muscio, the fact was, he was back at looking at a coronial inquiry as his only option.

～

After the tragic events of 2 June 2000, Tina, Judith Brown's neighbour, sought counselling to deal with the trauma she had suffered. Coincidentally, she saw the same counsellor from the Hunter New England Area Health Service who had dealt with Judith's three boys the night of the murder. Tina was the neighbour who, together with Beth, Ross had grabbed in a headlock and tried to force into the house to see Judith's body. Tina had wriggled free, but witnessed the effect Ross's actions had on Beth.

Tina had regular contact with the counsellor, talking over the events of the day that had become a nightmare for her, trying to come to terms with all she experienced and attempting to get her life back to normal. Although she had opened up about what had happened and how it affected her, there were still some things she kept to herself. During one visit to the counsellor, around July or August 2001, the burden Tina carried became too great. She had to tell someone about what had happened the day of Judith's murder. Tina was frightened, but she opened up to the counsellor. On hearing what Tina had to say, and having intimate knowledge of what had happened on 2 June 2000, the counsellor urged Tina to contact police. Tina agreed, although reluctantly. With Tina's permission, the counsellor phoned Peter Fox.

Peter was at his desk when the counsellor called, dealing with other crimes and still trying to put the brief together on Judith's murder for the coroner. Distracted with all he had to do, Peter didn't catch the urgency and gravity in the counsellor's voice. Despite being invited to meet with Tina, Peter said he could speak to her on the phone. This wasn't the first time a witness had called up to talk about the investigation. Tina had already given a statement to police on the day of the murder. It didn't really say much, other than she had never heard Ross and Judith argue and found them to be a normal family.

The counsellor became insistent and said it would be better if Peter visited Tina that day. What Tina had to say wasn't suitable to be relayed over the phone. Peter became struck with the seriousness of the situation and responded quickly.

Peter didn't want to get his hopes up. He'd been let down numerous times throughout the investigation, so whatever it was Tina had to say, Peter wasn't expecting it to be of great consequence. He drove to Nelson Bay where he met with the counsellor and Tina.

The meeting was difficult for Tina. She appeared frightened to Peter and very nervous. Studying her demeanour, Peter realised Tina had something important to tell him. This wasn't going to be a wasted trip, though the fact that she had waited fourteen months to come forward did frustrate Peter a little. She had better have a good reason, he thought.

Peter put his own feelings aside. He knew what Tina had been through on the day of the murder. She had witnessed Ross's violent outburst that afternoon, and Ross had tried to physically force her to see his wife's battered body. That day had taken its toll on Tina. She was obviously still shaken by the events, even all this time later. Peter sympathised with her and tried his best to make her feel relaxed.

Taking a breath Tina admitted to Peter she hadn't told police all she knew about Judith Brown's murder. She then said, 'I know Ross killed her'.

Peter was taken aback. 'How do you know? ... Did you see it, or what?'

Taking a moment to compose herself, Tina told her story.

On the Friday 2 June 2000 she had been at home watching a television program, *Good Morning Australia* with Bert Newton. The program began at 9.00 a.m. She had been watching for about 'five or ten minutes ... it might have been a bit longer, but not much'. Tina remembered the first commercial break was well under way. It was then she heard an argument taking place; the sound of it was coming from Ross and Judith's house. She heard a male voice and a female voice yelling at each other. Tina recognised Ross's voice and heard him shout, 'I have had a gutful of this crap'. The words were followed by a woman's scream, and then Ross yelled very loudly.

Peter accepted what Tina was saying as being truthful, because while she claimed to have heard Ross's voice, she admitted she couldn't be sure the female voice belonged to Judith. She hadn't really had much to do with Judith. Given all that was known, Tina could have easily assumed the voice was Judith's, but she wouldn't allow herself to make that claim. She would only tell Peter what she knew to be the facts. But how did she know it was Ross's voice?

It was put to Tina by Peter that people's voices change when they yell, so how could she be so certain it was Ross's voice? Tina explained that she had heard Ross on a number of occasions yelling at his boys in the backyard, or standing out the front of his house shouting for them to come home. She was very sure it was Ross's voice. It boomed through her house.

The reason Tina had heard Ross so clearly was because her son had broken the corner front window of their house, the one nearest the Brown residence, the day before. Tina had not been impressed, especially on the Friday when the wind blew through the hole, making it uncomfortably cold inside the house. She had been waiting for a glazier to arrive and fix the breakage.

Tina didn't want her neighbours knowing she had heard them arguing, so she switched off the television and started listening to her compact disc player: she put on a favourite song and turned the volume up. She played the song twice, to be sure it was enough time for the argument next door to be over. She hoped Ross and Judith would think she couldn't have heard anything over the music.

About fifteen or twenty minutes after hearing the shouting and screams, Tina heard the sound of a revving motor. As the sound was muffled by the music, she thought the motor belonged to her husband's vehicle. Tina's husband, Paul (not his real name), travelled interstate. When he did, he would be gone for days and arrive home at all hours. She quickly moved to the front window and opened the curtain to greet Paul. It wasn't her husband. Standing at the window she saw Ross's Toyota HiLux four-wheel-drive back out of the driveway and pass her house. Tina froze. She didn't see Ross in the vehicle, but was sure Ross had seen her.

Tina suffered from a vision impairment that made her eyes sensitive to light and prevented her from seeing the fine detail of objects at a distance, a condition she's had from birth. So how sure was she that it was Ross's four-wheel-drive she had seen?

Tina knew the sound of the HiLux, having heard it every day for the past six months after the Browns had moved in. When she was inside, the music distorted the sound, causing her to mistake it for her husband's vehicle. Standing at the window, however, Tina realised it was Ross's four-wheel-drive. Despite her poor eyesight, she even identified certain features of the vehicle, enough to satisfy Peter that she had actually seen it go past. While she could make out Ross's distinctive HiLux, she was unable to focus on the interior of the cabin.

'I cannot tell a lie,' she told Peter, 'I couldn't be sure it was Ross who was driving, but it was his truck.'

The time Tina had seen Ross leave his house was estimated at being between 9.25 and 9.30.

When Judith's workmate from the childcare centre knocked on her door, Tina was apprehensive about helping her. Tina was of the opinion that Ross and Judith had had an argument, and that Ross might have hit his wife. Tina admitted she had been a victim of domestic violence in her previous marriage and felt for Judith, imagining her sitting quietly and crying to herself, as she had done the same in the past.

Despite Judith's work colleague knocking on the Browns' door and ringing the bell, there was no answer. The two women could hear the radio in the house. When they went to the back door and found it open, Tina convinced the woman from the childcare centre not to enter, empathising with Judith's situation and wanting to leave her to herself. She thought Judith hadn't answered the door because she didn't want to see anyone. Tina used the excuse that she didn't know Judith well enough to just walk in.

From the sounds Tina heard she believed Judith had been assaulted, but never thought that her neighbour was a victim of a brutal slaying. Tina did think about calling the police soon after hearing the argument, but she knew from her own experience that little would have been achieved. She was sure it was just a domestic. Ross would tell police there was no problem, and Judith would have stood by her husband, as Tina had done when she was a victim. The police wouldn't have been able to do a thing.

In the afternoon, when she heard Ross screaming and shouting up and down the street, she went out to help. It took her a while to realise what was happening, but when she had worked out that Judith was dead, Ross grabbed her in a headlock and tried to force her to see Judith's body. Tina felt that Ross knew she had heard everything and was, perhaps, warning her to keep quiet. Continually, after this incident, she found Ross's general behaviour towards her threatening, which only convinced her of her suspicions.

Tina feared for her life and the lives of her children. After that day, Tina and her kids all slept in the same bedroom. She was scared of Ross and her children were fearful of some maniac lurking around the streets. Tina never told any of her family what she had witnessed that morning.

Even though Tina was obviously scared, the time it

had taken before Tina approached police with the whole story was of concern. Initially, as she had explained, she was fearful of Ross. A week or more later, however, Tina and her husband were approached by a member of an outlaw motorcycle gang, one of about a dozen such gangs in the Hunter region, who threatened the couple and warned them: 'I have word from the boss' mouth himself that if you open your mouth to the coppers about anything to do with Ross or Judith you will get a bullet in your head.'

The threat was taken seriously. Tina knew the gang member from the Anna Bay Tavern. She had seen Ross drinking with him on occasion and assumed the outlaw motorcycle gang was protecting Ross. She believed Ross had told his bikie friend that Tina had heard the argument and saw Ross leave the house that morning, and asked the motorcycle gang to warn Tina against giving any testimony.

Peter was amazed. He wondered if Ross had strong enough connections to get an outlaw motorcycle gang on side and have their protection. What also interested Peter was the name of the gang member. He was known as Jack, the same name as given by Ross to Henry and Phyllis as the name of Judith's alleged lover.

To verify the timing of Tina's statement, in which she claimed she had heard Ross during the first commercial break, Peter contacted Channel Ten, the host station for *Good Morning Australia*. The program is produced from Melbourne and broadcast nationally through its affiliates. Peter spoke to the Traffic

Department who schedule what commercials are played when and at what times. Though commercial breaks are given specified times, *Good Morning Australia* is a live-to-air program and the breaks can move by a few minutes, depending on what is happening on the show.

On Friday 2 June 2000, the program had begun at 9.00 a.m. with its opening credits, followed by Bert Newton's welcome, a rundown on what guests were appearing, introduction and short banter with the musical director John Foreman, and then the first guest interview. Bert Newton threw to a commercial break at just after 9.10.

This meant Tina's timings could be proven to say she had heard Ross's voice shouting at or soon after 9.10, well after the time he claimed to have left the house, but around the same time another neighbour, Danni, had stated she saw his four-wheel-drive parked in the driveway. Peter now had two witnesses who could testify that Ross was at home near the time Judith was murdered, which contradicted his record of interview.

In addition to Tina's time being corroborated by the television station, the fact she had heard shouting, a woman's scream, and then Ross yelling, fitted in with the approximate time police believed Judith had been attacked. Judith's watch had stopped at 9.14.28, which meant Tina had probably heard the initial attack, before Judith was battered with the swagman statue. The information Tina gave police was considered very credible because police had never disclosed anything about the watch. There was no way Tina could have known her timings would correlate with the time Judith's watch had ceased to work.

The other factor that convinced Peter of what Tina had told him was the phrase she heard Ross use: 'I've had a gutful of this crap'. Peter remembered that another neighbour quoted exactly those words as being used by Ross when he was prancing and screaming up and down the street. It was obviously a phrase commonly used by Ross, one also used when Peter spoke to him later that day.

Hearing Tina's statement, Peter's hope of getting a conviction increased considerably. It was the missing link that helped corroborate other evidence Peter had against Ross Brown. For Peter, putting Tina's statement together with the rest of the evidence meant he was on his way to arresting Ross. But, still fearful of the threat against her life, Tina refused to make a formal statement. Peter assured her he would give her protection and look into the matter. Tina wasn't convinced. It was too big a risk for her to take.

Peter would now have to locate Jack and have a talk with the outlaw motorcycle gang to ascertain what involvement they had with Ross and why, if it were true, they were protecting what he had done to Judith. Then, if he was to get Tina's help, he would have to convince her she and her family would be safe.

～◦

As it happened, Peter Fox was investigating a bikie gang war that had recently broken out among two rival gangs, the local chapters of the Bandido and the Gypsy

Jokers. In March the president of the Bandido Motorcycle Club, Rodney Partington, had tried to plant a hand-made bomb at the Gypsy Jokers' clubhouse, situated on an industrial estate at Weston. The clubhouse was protected with a high fence, barbed wire, and electronic surveillance. Partington had cut a hole in the fence to gain access, but something had gone wrong and the Bandidos' president died when the bomb exploded in his hands. It was presumed Partington had planned to plant the bomb in retaliation, believing the Gypsy Jokers had fired shots at the Abermain home of a Bandido member four weeks earlier, and for fire bombing a tattoo parlour owned by Partington in Kurri Kurri.

During March the bikie war escalated. Members of each club became involved in violent attacks across the Lower Hunter. Other outlaw motorcycle gangs joined in the fracas. Police formed Strike Force Tanfield to try to quell the violence and get the gangs to resolve their differences. As Peter Fox told the *Newcastle Herald* on 28 March, 'It's not a secret that they [the bikies] are a very difficult group to try and work with, but we are trying to work with them ... If we can facilitate that [a resolution] and help a little bit, all the better.'

In June, after members of a third gang were seriously assaulted at a bakery in broad daylight and a reprisal attack was launched on a bikie-owned business during shopping hours, police launched coordinated raids on club members across Newcastle and the Lower Hunter regions. Police confiscated drugs and firearms. The operation resulted in only one man being charged with affray and assault occasioning bodily harm.

This wasn't the first time Peter had had involvement with members of outlaw motorcycle gangs. He'd been involved in other operations where he'd broken up their illegal activities. There were occasions when, even though he knew what they were up to, all he could do was give them warnings because he did not have the evidence to lock them away. Because of his past dealings, and with recent events, Peter had a list of contact telephone numbers for the hierarchy of each of the outlaw motorcycle gangs operating in the Lower Hunter.

Between working with his colleagues to try to stop an all out gang war, and putting together the case against Ross Brown, Peter finally tracked down Jack, the outlaw motorcycle club gang member and informed him that he was wanted for questioning. Jack attended Maitland Police Station with the secretary of the motorcycle club, who was a little puzzled as to why police had become so interested in one of their members. Before Peter explained, he asked if the secretary knew Ross Brown. The response gave Peter his answer: 'Who the fuck is Ross Brown?'

Peter explained the reasons for needing to talk with Jack: the murder of Judith Brown, her husband being the prime suspect, and the threat made by Jack against Tina and her husband after the murder. Knowing bikies as well as he did, Peter knew he wouldn't get any information from them if it meant they would have to admit to being involved in illegal activities. Peter assured the secretary he wasn't interested in anything other than wanting to know if Jack had threatened Tina on behalf of Ross and what did Jack know of the murder. Had Ross said anything about killing Judith to him?

In Peter's words, 'We're not after you for anything at the moment. I don't know what you're up to, I know you're up to something, you always are. That's the game we play. I'm putting that aside for the moment. All I'm worried about is this murder and why Jack has gone up … I believe he's made threats to a particular witness … I don't want to screw you over anything else; I'll save that for another day.'

The secretary wasn't happy; his club didn't need this attention from the police, particularly when it involved a murder. He decided to accept as genuine what Peter was saying: whatever Jack was into would be put to one side in favour of information relating to Ross Brown. He told Peter to give him five minutes and he left and had a quiet word with Jack.

After some time the secretary returned. He was somewhat relieved to tell Peter no one in the club other than Jack knew Ross Brown. Jack didn't know Tina had any information regarding the murder, and Jack had acted alone, without the knowledge of or any support from the club. It was all a misunderstanding, and the club was sorry Jack had caused a problem for the police and their witness. As though acting out a scene in a British crime drama-comedy, the club secretary then began speaking cryptically about the threat and particular 'business dealings' Jack might have had with Ross Brown, all of which was, of course, off the record.

The club secretary suggested that the threat 'may' have happened, and if it had, it was only done in relation to business dealings that might have occurred between Jack and Ross Brown. Jack was totally unaware of Ross's involvement in Judith's murder. He would never have interfered in such a serious police investigation. It is possible, though, that Jack was aware, given Judith's murder, that police would be speaking with Tina and her husband about Ross. Of course, Jack didn't want the couple saying anything about the club or any business the club or Jack had with Ross, so Jack decided to warn Tina and her husband not to say anything. Strictly concerning the business, of course. While the threat was a little heavy handed, it was all down to Jack. The club did not endorse the threat or know that Jack had made it. At the same time, Jack would not have known what Tina knew about the murder. He did not mean for Tina not to tell police what she knew of the murder, just for her not to say anything about any business dealings.

Without saying so directly, the secretary had admitted that Ross was buying drugs from Jack at the Anna Bay Tavern. Tina and her husband were regular drinkers at the Tavern as well, and would most likely have known of Jack's business dealings. By the end of discussions, Peter was left in no doubt that neither Jack nor any other member of the motorcycle club would be giving evidence concerning the supply of drugs to Ross Brown.

The club secretary agreed to allow Jack to make a statement, but only under certain conditions. He didn't want the club's name being mentioned and he didn't want its reputation soiled.

Jack admitted to knowing Ross Brown. They had known each other for about twenty years from when they were kids growing up together at Wallsend. They used to ride Triumph motorcycles back then. Jack had been drinking with Ross on the day of the murder at the Anna Bay Tavern. As with other patrons who knew Ross, Jack hadn't noticed anything out of character in Ross's behaviour. He seemed his normal self, though he was drinking more than he usually would on a weekday. Jack denied knowing Judith. Obviously, he knew of her, but was not having an affair with Ross's wife. He recalled one time when Ross had invited him home for a drink and almost immediately Judith had yelled at Ross to get 'his mate' out of the house. Judith did not appreciate having a bikie under her roof.

During the statement, Jack refused to make any mention of his motorcycle club, as agreed, and did not give any details or make admissions regarding the threat against Tina and her husband. Jack was not giving any information that would incriminate him.

After the statement was taken, the club secretary told Peter to tell Tina that she had his word, on behalf of the club, that no harm would come to her or any of her family if she gave evidence against Ross, providing, of course, she kept her testimony to what she knew about that Friday morning. 'We really don't need this shit,' the secretary assured Peter.

Peter contacted Tina and explained what Jack had to say about the threat. Tina knew of Jack's dealings but had been unaware that Ross was purchasing drugs. While Peter assured Tina and her husband of their safety, Tina was still shaken by everything she had been through. Despite still being apprehensive, she had to put an end to it. Tina finally agreed to give evidence against Ross and returned to the station and made a formal statement.

It took Peter some time to bring Tina around. He explained to her that her testimony would be the key in getting a successful conviction against Ross. What she knew would put him away for a long time. Tina didn't think anyone would believe her because she had taken so long to come forward. Peter knew that that was a problem, but accepted that she had good reason to be scared. He understood why she had waited so long and felt a jury would also sympathise with the mother of three. Her evidence would be what mattered. Peter needed Tina to take a chance. He offered her and her family police protection, but she declined. She wasn't going to hide. She was sick of living in fear.

Further enquiries by police to try and identify the Jack mentioned by Ross as being the man who was having an affair with Judith came up empty. Peter never found anyone admitting to having an affair with Judith, or anyone else who could corroborate Ross's allegation. As Peter had thought, Ross, for whatever reason, had made up the story about his wife's infidelity.

Chapter 10

AGAINST THE ODDS

Over the following months from when Tina had revealed her knowledge of what she heard and saw the morning of Judith Brown's murder, Peter Fox carefully reviewed all the evidence he had against Ross Brown. He wanted to be sure. He wanted to be in no doubt that Ross had killed his wife and that he had the evidence to prove it. As determined as Peter was in wanting to resolve the case, to give the families answers to how and why Judith died, and as much as everything pointed to Ross as the perpetrator, Peter was still being objective in his evaluation of the evidence. He didn't want to put away an innocent man.

In addition to reviewing the evidence, Peter also kept an eye on Ross. In particular, Peter was still receiving updates on Ross's finances. In October 2000, the Supreme Court finally granted Ross access to Judith's fixed term account, which totalled $117 847.68. Around the same time, Ross also tried to get hold of Judith's superannuation fund, but Judith's father intervened, requesting the money be held in a trust account for the three boys. Judith's father was successful and the money was put aside to be divided equally between Riley, Joel and Gene.

Between 27 October 2000 and 15 March 2001, less than five months, Ross spent more than $96 000 from the fixed term account. In March, as the money dwindled away, Ross approached Murray for a loan. Ross went to him crying and said, 'I've just finished paying off some bills and I am flat broke. I need the money for my boys, food and stuff like that.'

Feeling sorry for Ross, Murray lent him $200. In April 2001 Ross wrote a letter to Coalsuper Services requesting they release funds from his super because of hardship. He wrote that, 'of the $12 000 I had at the time Judy died there is nothing left … I beg that you consider my situation. It is not easy to cope at all with everything that has happened but my financial situation is only adding to the stress … Access to this money will give myself and my boys some hope for the future.'

Interestingly, Ross made no mention of the fact he had access to, and had spent by the time he wrote this letter, well over $100 000 from Judith's estate. The $12 000 Ross referred to in the letter is believed to have been the money in the joint accounts he exhausted prior to the murder. As a result of Ross's letter, Coalsuper Services paid out $7850.00 to Ross on 4 May 2001 from the preserved portion of his superannuation. Within eighteen days, on 21 May 2001, only $1.61 of the super money remained.

On 11 July 2001 Ross received a compensation payment from Coal Miners Insurance for $61 633.18. After two months and ten days, on 20 September 2001, only $14.77 remained in the account. During this time

Ross and the boys had moved to a Housing Commission property in Blaxland Avenue, Singleton Heights. Peter had also been informed that Ross continued to be a regular visitor at the home of the known drug dealer mentioned earlier, the same drug dealer Peter had arrested and convicted using covert surveillance.

Sitting down with pen and paper, Peter calculated that Ross had acquired $211 394.18 since Judith's murder, and there was nothing to show for it in any bank account. It was also known that Ross had not purchased any furnishings or belongings that could be attributed to the amount spent. Averaging Ross's spending habits over the time from July 2000, it showed he had been spending more than $13 000 a month. This didn't include regular payments Ross received in the way of unemployment benefits, and family and youth allowances that totalled a fortnightly income of $961.62.

Peter still believed that money was a strong possible motivator for Ross to have killed Judith. Quite possibly, as he had theorised, Ross and Judith argued over the family finances that Friday morning, and with anger building up inside, Ross decided he had 'had a gutful' and struck out at his wife. There was no doubt in Peter's mind that he had his man and Ross would be brought to justice. How soon would depend on the strength of his brief of evidence.

Peter checked all the evidence thoroughly. He continued running ideas past Peter Muscio just in case there was anything more they felt they could extract from the physical evidence. As far as the physical evidence was concerned, it was agreed they had done all they could. There was still a possibility, however faint, that other witnesses might come forward. Peter considered this, but looking at the evidence he had, including Tina's statement along with those given by Danni, Phyllis and Henry, he believed he had all he needed.

Putting everything together—Ross's inconsistencies over the beer bottles, witnesses putting him at the house after 9.00 a.m, his behaviour that revealed a lack of emotion or grief over his wife's death, Judith's concerns over the family's financial situation, his erratic spending, his drug habit, and Tina having heard Ross arguing and a woman's scream around the time Judith's watch had stopped working—Peter sat back and said to himself, 'I've got him'.

To be sure, Peter ran the evidence past some of his colleagues. He wanted their advice, wanted them to play devil's advocate, to try to find holes in his case. While Peter's hard work was recognised, not all of his fellow officers shared his optimism about achieving a conviction. One factor was the amount of time it had taken for Peter's key witness, Tina, to come forward. They were concerned it wouldn't look good to a jury, and that Tina might be portrayed as an unreliable witness. After all, how good is a person's memory after fourteen months?

Peter understood their scepticism, though he didn't

agree. He wasn't being stubborn; it was just that, having spoken with Tina, he accepted her as a credible witness, despite the time it had taken her to contact police. She had good reason to remember the day well. Everything that happened that day had become a nightmare for her and her family. She also had a good reason for taking her time. Anyone believing their life and the lives of their family were in danger would be a little hesitant in talking.

Then there was Ross. Without a confession, or Ross agreeing to talk with Peter again, his colleagues thought Peter's brief was too weak and he could lose at a trial.

The advice Peter received was to hold off arresting Ross and run the evidence at a coronial inquest, as he had planned to do. The inquest would naturally come to the same conclusion as Peter had, pointing to Ross as the perpetrator, and it might help flush out other evidence that would strengthen the prosecution case. Peter wasn't convinced. He had already decided that he had all the evidence he was going to collect. It had been almost eighteen months and, apart from Tina, no one had come forward with any substantial information. He didn't believe there was anyone else out there who could place Ross in the house at the time of the murder. It was also of concern to Peter than an inquest could drag the matter out even longer, testing witnesses' memories. Presenting evidence at an inquest could delay any chance of a trial by up to a year.

The other problem for Peter was that he would have to reveal everything he had against Ross at the inquest.

Unlike a committal hearing, an inquest cannot refer the evidence to trial. Peter feared this would give Ross the upper hand. Ross would then be aware of all the police had and be given the time to come up with excuses to counter the evidence and witness statements. If nothing new developed after the inquest, then Peter's job of convicting Ross for murder could possibly be made harder.

Peter still had only a circumstantial case against Ross. No one had seen him kill Judith, and some of the physical evidence could be argued to support the case against Ross or support Ross's version of events. Each piece of evidence on its own meant little, but when put together they created a whole picture that showed Ross as the only person to have had the opportunity to kill Judith.

In some homicide cases police will send their brief of evidence to the DPP. It is the DPP who has the job of presenting and arguing the evidence in court. It is the DPP who must convince a jury of the defendant's guilt based on the strength of evidence collected by the investigating police, which is why some police seek the DPP's advice before committing themselves to an arrest. Peter decided not to go to the DPP first. He already knew it, like his colleagues, would most likely recommend more evidence be obtained.

Nonetheless, it would be Peter's call. It was his case. He'd collected the evidence and knew the case better than anyone. He would decide if Ross was to be arrested or not. Peter was certain there was no more evidence to be found. Despite the advice, he believed he had enough to charge Ross. After for a few days considering the advice and what options were available to him, he made the decision to let a jury decide if his evidence was strong enough to convict Ross. It was crunch time.

In Peter's words: 'I bounced it [the evidence] off a lot of people, but I thought in the end, bugger it, if I get kicked in the arse, I get kicked in the arse ... I'll just wear it.'

Early on the morning of 27 November 2001, Peter Fox and another detective from Maitland, Peter Birch, drove to Singleton to arrest Ross Brown. Peter Fox stands tall, and together with Peter Birch, who had a solid build, the two men looked quite a formidable duo. Peter Fox was happy with his choice of partner, chosen just in case Ross objected to being arrested. This was the moment Peter had been waiting for. He imagined how he would feel taking Ross into custody. It had been a long time and he knew he would feel elated.

The two men sat in an unmarked police vehicle keeping watch on Ross's Blaxland Avenue house. Peter was fully aware of Ross's daily routine, which started with taking one of his boys to school. Local police had tracked Ross's movements and passed on their observations to Peter in anticipation of an arrest.

Peter didn't want to take Ross into custody in front of his children. They'd been through enough. Knowing their father had been arrested for the murder of their mother would be enough of a shock for them; Peter didn't want to add to their trauma by having them witness his arrest. Since Judith's murder, Ross and his three boys had become inseparable. Peter had no doubt that they had formed a close bond and that the boys would be the last to believe their father was guilty. No matter what other relatives or family friends suspected, Peter knew the boys would be Ross's staunchest supporters.

Ross emerged from his house and proceeded to a local school where he dropped off his son. From there, Ross travelled into Singleton and parked outside a chemist shop to collect his methadone prescription. The chemist would serve the prescribed dosage to Ross at the counter. As soon as Ross stepped into the shop, the two detectives alighted from their vehicle and followed him in. While Ross waited at the counter for his prescription, Peter Fox tapped him on the shoulder and said, 'Ross Brown, I want to advise you you're under arrest for the murder of your wife, Judith Brown, on the second of June 2000'.

Ross's jaw dropped. 'You're fucking kidding.'

Peter remembered that he felt no buzz, no elation. All he felt was an anticlimax. After all the work and the hours spent building to this moment, Peter was hit with the realisation that it wasn't over. If anything, it had just begun. Arresting Ross meant Peter's evidence would come under close scrutiny.

If a jury wasn't convinced and Ross walked a free man, then all of Peter's work, and the work of all his colleagues who assisted in the investigation, would have been for nothing. Peter had no doubt about Ross's guilt, but now he wondered if he had enough to see it through. He wasn't doubting himself or the strength of his evidence, but he knew the judicial system and began questioning if all his evidence would be allowed.

It wouldn't be the first time that, because of legal argument and much to the angst of police and the prosecution, a trial judge had thrown out evidence. In any brief of evidence, certain aspects can be argued by the defence to be prejudicial or irrelevant. Peter began thinking about his evidence and the likelihood that some of it might not be admissible. If it was, would there be enough left to convict Ross Brown of murder?

The two detectives bundled Ross into their car and transported him to Singleton Police Station. It was arranged with the chemist for police to collect Ross's methadone and give it to him at a later time. Charging Ross with murder had become the priority.

At Singleton Police Station Ross was formally charged. He contacted his solicitor, who informed Peter that his client would not be making any statement. Peter expected little else. Arrangements were made for the three boys to be taken into the care of their paternal aunt, the same aunt who had lent police her statue of the swagman.

During a quiet moment, Peter had a talk with Ross. 'We're going to give you a run for it, Ross,' he said.

'But, I didn't do it, Pete.'

'Mate, I think you did. You're going to tell me you

didn't. Ultimately, at the end of the day, the decision is going to be made by a judge and a jury, not by you and me talking here in the police station. I know you're never going to admit to it. You know you're never going to admit to it. I don't expect anything different, but I think I've got enough to run you. If the jury says you haven't done it, so be it. I'll wear that. I might not like it, but that's the reality. That's why we have courts.'

Once Ross had been formally processed, he was taken to Singleton Local Court where he stood in the dock and appeared before a magistrate. The police duty prosecutor, Sergeant Danny Maher, summarised the case against Ross, saying that police alleged that he had killed Judith to access money to feed a drug habit.

Sergeant Maher then outlined the case. He said it was a 'strong case' and that police had accounts from witnesses who placed Ross in the house after the murder. It was also revealed that Ross's version of events on the Friday of the murder conflicted with testimony given by various witnesses. According to Sergeant Maher, the financial benefit Ross gained after his wife's death was a motive for the killing, and he explained that Ross had spent a considerable amount of money since Judith's death on his drug addiction.

Ross's solicitor, Daniel Smyth, maintained his client's innocence and denied the police allegations. 'There is absolutely no evidence or motive that he gained one cent from the death of his wife.'

Requesting that Ross be granted bail, Mr Smyth argued the prosecution case was like a 'house of cards'.

He described the evidence against Ross as a 'purely speculative set of propositions', and, under close scrutiny, would show there was 'very little' evidence.

Opposing bail, Sergeant Maher detailed the events of 2 June 2000 and the contact police had had with Ross Brown following the murder. More detail came out about Ross's finances. It was mentioned Ross had spent $12 000 prior to the murder and that he had 'exhausted in excess of $200 000 in cash and other property' since the murder.

The magistrate refused bail and remanded Ross in custody. Ross appeared at Newcastle Local Court on 5 December 2001 in a second attempt for bail. This time, Peter Fox addressed the court, explaining to Magistrate Sharron Crews that the prosecution had served 174 documents on the defence, and that the evidence against Ross Brown was a 'strong circumstantial case'.

Again the magistrate refused bail. Ross Brown would spend Christmas 2001 on remand. It was expected that a committal hearing would be held early in the new year.

As Peter expected, with Ross now behind bars, his work had just commenced. There was no knowing what, of all his evidence, would be allowed at the trial and what would be rejected. That was a problem he and the DPP would have to deal with when the time came. Peter's immediate problem came from some of the witnesses who were to give the evidence.

Once Ross had been arrested, the reality of what

they had committed themselves to hit home. Nerves grew and people became worried about repercussions, especially if Ross walked free. Peter spent hours talking to some witnesses, building their confidence, making them aware of their importance to the prosecution. A circumstantial case relies on the totality of the evidence and not on any single part. Peter knew his case wasn't reliant on any one witness, but rather on all the witnesses telling their individual stories. Even though Tina put Ross in the house at the time of the murder, it meant nothing without other evidence to show Ross's deception and the obvious lies he told in trying to distance himself from the murder.

Peter had come a long way. If success was dependent on him spending his own time listening to the concerns of witnesses, then so be it.

Chapter 11

A CASE TO ANSWER

Ross Brown was granted bail on 6 April 2002. His solicitor for the bail application, Margaret Zahra, described the prosecution case as purely circumstantial and a 'hotchpotch of nonsense'. She told Magistrate Alan Railton that her client had strong ties to the area, was close to his three sons, and that they missed him desperately. His ties to the community and the relationship that existed between father and sons meant he would not try to make a break for it.

The magistrate accepted the application and noted that Ross did not have a 'particularly excessive criminal record'. While granting bail, Magistrate Alan Railton did place conditions on Ross: he was to reside in Tanilba Bay with Paula, his stepmother, and there would be a self-surety of $100 000, with an additional $30 000 to be deposited by his stepmother. Of course he was not to approach any witnesses.

As for when a committal hearing would begin, it was hoped one might get underway mid year, but the scheduling of courts is a very complex exercise and an exact date was never given.

While waiting for a date for the committal hearing, Peter Fox decided to take matters into his own hands. The DPP had Peter's brief of evidence and, in time would assign the case to an available solicitor and barrister. As it was, the DPP had already assigned solicitor Christine Hunter to the case. Peter was more than happy to be working with Christine Hunter, but he couldn't stop himself from being anxious over who would be assigned as the prosecuting barrister.

In an unprecedented move, Peter went to the DPP offices and requested a specific barrister for the case. He wanted Wayne Creasey and didn't want to wait for the DPP to assign just any Crown barrister. Naturally, the officials at the DPP were curious about Peter's request. They wanted an explanation before deciding whether Peter would get his man.

Peter knew Wayne Creasey. They had worked together on other cases and Peter had been impressed by Wayne's attention to detail, his rapport with witnesses, and his courtroom charisma. He was softly spoken but commanded attention when he addressed a court. People naturally warmed to Wayne; he was that sort of person. Peter Fox wanted the best, and he believed Wayne was the best.

Courtrooms are places of high drama, with lots of stoppages while counsels argue over the finer points of law. Peter was of the opinion he would win or lose the trial not just on the evidence, but on how that evidence was presented to the jury. Prosecution and defence counsels must both get their arguments across to the jury succinctly, in a sequence that holds their attention, and that makes it easy to follow, so that nothing is lost by way of delays, stoppages, or excessive use of legal jargon. If Peter were to lose, he didn't want to lose without giving it his best shot. Wayne Creasey was his best shot.

The DPP considered Peter's request. It was the first time in Peter's experience any police officer had made such a demand. As it turned out, Peter got his way: Wayne Creasey agreed to prosecute Ross Brown and the DPP scheduled him for the committal and subsequent trial.

⌐

The committal hearing got underway at the Newcastle Local Court on 10 December 2002, just over two and half years after Judith's murder. In some cases the committal can become a mini trial, with the prosecution, or the Crown, as it is referred to, calling witnesses to give their testimony in person. In this instance, it was a paper hearing—all the statements and evidence were submitted to Magistrate Stephen Jackson for consideration.

Counsel for the Crown, Wayne Creasey, addressed the court, explaining that the prosecution case against Ross Brown was entirely circumstantial. He went on to say that the evidence would establish the time of Mrs Brown's death was around 9.15 a.m. and that a blunt instrument, the swagman statue used by the family as a doorstop, was the most likely murder weapon.

Solicitor Margaret Zahra argued, as she had done in her bail application, that Ross Brown was innocent of the charges and that the case against her client 'did not even get to the prima facie level', which literally means 'at first sight' or 'on the face of it'. This meant that Ms Zahra didn't accept that the evidence would convict Ross, even before undergoing any scrutiny by the defence.

Although the committal was mostly a presentation of the evidence on paper, Tina was called to give her testimony. Very calmly, Tina went through her evidence. She recalled hearing Ross's voice and a woman's scream; she accounted for the time she heard the argument and, most importantly to her, she got to explain the reason why she had waited fourteen months to speak to police.

The hearing was halted for the Christmas and New Year break and to give Magistrate Jackson time to read and digest all the documented evidence.

The committal hearing resumed on 25 February 2003. Having read all the tendered documents, the magistrate felt there was evidence capable of satisfying a jury beyond reasonable doubt. Ross Brown did have a case to answer and was committed to trial in the Newcastle Supreme Court.

Magistrate Jackson allowed Ross to remain on bail, provided he adhered to the conditions that had been set earlier.

The outcome was no surprise to either side. It is rare, though not unheard of, for a case to be thrown out at the committal stage. While all the evidence, including Ross's financial records and known drug habit, was submitted in the committal hearing, there was no way of knowing how much of the evidence would see its way to trial. It wouldn't be unusual for the defence counsel to try to stop some evidence, which can include witnesses, from being presented.

The committal hearing was a straightforward affair. Peter Fox wasn't as concerned about the hearing as he was about the trial. His concern, however, would deepen after the first day of the committal.

On 28 December 2002, Tina's husband, Paul, was having a drink at the Anna Bay Tavern. He was reportedly enjoying his time when members of an outlaw motorcycle gang pounced him and assaulted him. They were members of the same motorcycle gang that Jack had been affiliated with.

Tina and Paul both assumed that the assault was in response to Tina having given evidence at the committal. After all, Tina's appearance and testimony had been widely reported in the local media. They contacted Peter Fox, who couldn't believe what he was hearing. Here was his key witness, already on the edge as it was, and then her husband found himself being beaten by gang members who had made an earlier threat against their life. This was all Peter needed.

Peter immediately went and spoke with the secretary of the outlaw motorcycle gang. The secretary informed Peter the assault was a mistake over an unrelated matter. It had nothing to do with Ross Brown or the murder. The secretary apologised once more for the misunderstanding and promised it wouldn't occur again. Peter had his word.

After Peter spent some time with Tina and Paul, the couple agreed to continue with giving their testimony. In fact, they made an additional statement regarding the initial threat and were prepared to give evidence in court on the matter. After Peter explained about the recent 'mistake' at the Anna Bay Tavern, Paul accepted Peter's advice to stop frequenting the Tavern to avoid future encounters with the outlaw motorcycle gang members. Paul didn't want any more trouble and neither did Peter.

Peter now just had to concentrate on the trial. He would spend time with Christine Hunter and Wayne Creasey to make sure everything and everyone was ready for the big day. As Peter had said, if he did lose, he didn't want to lose for lack of trying.

Chapter 12

JUDGMENT DAY

Preparing for a trial isn't as easy as handing over all the documented evidence and statements to the Director of Public Prosecutions and letting them argue it in court. Police work with the prosecution team to provide supporting material, such as maps, diagrams, and photos, to help the Crown give the jury a picture of what happened, how it happened, and who was responsible.

In the months leading up to the trial of Ross Brown, Peter Fox, Peter Muscio, Christine Hunter, and Wayne Creasey all worked together to make sure that every aspect of the prosecution case would be easily understood and had supporting material when needed. Everything was cross-checked and Peter Fox made sure the witnesses were comfortable and ready to give their testimony. In some instances, he even arranged for other officers to collect the witness, sit with them through court, and then deliver them home. Peter wanted to be sure they felt safe and secure.

The day finally arrived. Friends and relatives of Judith and Ross filed into the Newcastle Supreme Court on 27 October 2003. Before proceedings officially got under way, Justice Robert Hulme heard legal arguments from both sides. As had been arranged, Wayne Creasey represented the Crown, while Carolyn Davenport appeared for the defence. The issues raised before Justice Hulme were the financial records relating to Ross's spending, his known drug habit and use of methadone, the tape recordings made by Phyllis and Henry, and the right of the Crown to call Ross's three boys and stepmother as witnesses for the prosecution.

In the absence of a jury, both sides gave arguments as to why these issues should be included and why they should be excluded. Ultimately, the decision on each of the issues rested with the trial judge. After hearing all the Crown and the defence had to say, Justice Hulme made his ruling.

With regards to Ross's financial situation, the judge decided that Ross's spending patterns after Judith's death was not compelling enough to be presented as evidence for the prosecution. It could not be shown to relate to a motive or have a consequence leading to Judith's death. Indeed, it could be considered prejudicial. This meant Justice Hulme felt that while Ross's spendthrift nature might cause the jury to see him in a bad light, it did not mean he had killed his wife.

The judge gave a similar ruling on Ross's drug habit. Again, Justice Hulme believed this part of Ross's life, if presented to the jury, could be prejudicial, but did not mean he was a killer. Any mention of Ross's drug use, the methadone program, and his associations with suppliers and other users was ruled out. The judge wanted Ross tried on the facts leading up to and including the day of Judith's murder. He didn't want Ross being judged on being a drug addict or a poor handler of money.

For Peter Fox this ruling was a big blow. He'd spent the last six months putting together graphs and documents detailing Ross's spending since the murder. Peter had always believed Ross's motivation for murdering Judith was to access money to feed his habit, and as far as Peter was concerned, Ross's excessive spending after Judith's death proved this. Justice Hulme's ruling was seen by Peter as putting a big hole in the prosecution case; however, it was not an uncommon ruling and was something police and the prosecution would have to accept.

There was a win of sorts for the Crown. Justice Hulme decided the recordings made by Phyllis and Henry would not be played to the jury. He didn't want to rule on their illegality or not; that wasn't the issue. No reference could be made by either the Crown or defence to the jury of the tapes' existence. He did rule, though, that there was nothing stopping Phyllis and Henry giving testimony to what was said by Ross without referring to the tapes. Justice Hulme also added that, given there was a recording to verify what was said in conversation, the defence could not cross-examine either Phyllis or Henry on the truthfulness of the conversations, which meant the defence had to accept, without argument, Phyllis and Henry's recollection of the conversations they had had with Ross between April and May 2001.

When preparing for the trial the Crown decided to call Ross's three boys and Paula as witnesses for the prosecution, particularly as Joel's record of interview contradicted Ross's story for the morning of the murder. Justice Hulme rejected the submission. They were the defendant's family members and as such had the right to chose if they wanted to give evidence. None of their evidence would be allowed without the permission of the defence. Needless to say, the defence, on behalf of the family, declined.

After the ground rules had been set, a jury of nine men and three women took their places. The trial then began. It was to take six weeks and at least seventy witnesses would be called by the Crown to give evidence.

The jury heard from one of the paramedics who was first on the scene, who described Judith's injuries as the worst he had ever seen. Jury members were taken through the evidence relating to the watch, how it had stopped because of being struck during the attack and blood seeping into the works. Most importantly, the jury was shown the time the watch had stopped, 9.14.28, the time when Judith was believed to have been assaulted.

Detective Senior Constable Peter Muscio and Forensic Pathologist Doctor Tim Lyons appeared during the following two days. Peter went through the physical evidence collected at the scene, including the blood discovered in Ross's four-wheel-drive and samples of blood, hair, glass fragments, and cement residue taken during the autopsy. More than 120 items had been sent for forensic analysis.

Photos from the crime scene were also submitted. A photo of the bloody circular pattern on top of the dividing wall was shown to the jury, who were told that it was considered to have been made by the bottom of a beer bottle after the bottle had been placed in the blood. This was shown as contradicting Ross's story that he had immediately dropped the two bottles of beer when he entered the house. The circular mark was evidence that at least one of the bottles was placed on the partition before being broken.

It was also emphasised that Peter and the other Crime Scene examiners did not find any evidence to support the possibility that a break-in had occurred.

On cross-examination, Carolyn Davenport insinuated that Peter had manipulated the physical evidence to suit Peter Fox in his pursuit of Ross Brown. Peter Muscio denied it. The facts were the facts and there was little anyone could do to change that. Muscio also came under fire over hair samples he had taken from Judith's hands during the autopsy.

Initially, when the hair was discovered in Judith's palms, Peter sent the samples off for DNA analysis, but this was unsuccessful as there was no root attached to the hair, making it impossible to know to whom the hair belonged. Carolyn Davenport asked Peter why he didn't check for hair comparison to find out if the hair could have come from Ross or Judith or a third person.

Peter didn't consider hair analysis because the process doesn't identify any one person. It isn't particular evidence. Hair comparison can only say if the hair sample doesn't match another. Carolyn Davenport requested a comparison be done on the hairs from Judith's palm against those of her client and those known to belong to Judith. It was arranged for the Analytical Laboratory in Lidcombe to conduct the test.

Peter admitted he hadn't found any signs of blood that belonged to Ross in any of the basins, the shower, or bath. There was no evidence to conclude anyone had tried to remove blood from their body or clothing. The defence were countering the prosecution's suggestion that Ross had cleaned himself up after killing Judith and before leaving for the beach and the Anna Bay Tavern.

Tim Lyons detailed the horrific injuries Judith had suffered at the hands of her killer. He explained that the cuts and bruising to her fingers and forearms were typical defence wounds, and that Judith, although in vain, had tried to protect herself. He concluded that Judith had been struck on the head at least twice with the murder weapon, a heavy object that was most likely the swagman statue the family kept as a doorstop. 'The injuries I observed were extremely major head injuries that I think would have rapidly and inevitably led to death.'

When it came time for the witnesses, most were nervous but they all delivered their testimony without any great difficulty. The jury heard how, on the afternoon of the murder, Ross shouted obscenities at ambulance and police officers, had tried to drag his neighbours, Tina and Beth, by the head to see his dead wife, smeared blood over his face and body, and punched and head butted walls. Earlier that afternoon, Ross had been drinking at the Tavern and 'just seemed like himself', 'relaxed and joking', and 'did not seem nervous or on edge or anything'. It was made clear to the jury that Judith ran the family finances as money seemed to slip through Ross's hands 'like sand'.

To show that Ross couldn't be trusted with money, the prosecution introduced a witness who testified to the time when Ross had put a couple of thousand dollars through a poker machine in one night. When Judith found out she kicked him out of the house. Eventually, he returned, only to be forced to live in the garage until Judith calmed down.

The jury heard how, after Ross had accepted redundancy, his attitude towards Judith was one of 'he had worked all his life and now it was her turn'. The calls to the bank to enquire about having the fixed term deposit changed from being in Judith's name only to his name, including him telling the bank officer that 'there's some funny business going on', was all presented to court.

In addition, the prosecution called a woman from Centrelink who, on 29 May 2000, four days before the murder, spoke with Ross about rates of payment he and his wife would receive. In her words Ross was 'very short and very agitated', and after she explained what portion of the benefits would go to Judith and what to Ross, he commented, 'She gets all the money and I get nothing'.

The jury heard about Ross's Tanilba Bay house and how he took pride in the fact that it was his and that

Judith received nothing from its income. Then came the fact that the shared account was overdrawn just days before the murder and the rent on the Clonmeen Circuit house had not been paid, despite Ross contacting the real estate agent and promising to pay.

Phyllis and Henry were able to tell the jury of the conversation they had had with Ross in which he told them of his suspicion that Judith was having an affair with a younger man. Their testimony, as directed by Justice Hulme, was given without any objection or challenge by the defence. To any jury member who had previously served on a jury, this must have appeared strange. Any recollection of what was said during a conversation is usually down to one person's word against another's. It is easy for a defence counsel to suggest a witness may have selective memory and rebut their version. In this instance, there was a recording, though the jury was never made aware of its existence.

Tina had a harder time of it. She was very nervous. Sitting in the witness box, with all eyes focused on her, Tina became shaky and couldn't express herself as well as she had when talking with Peter back in August 2001. Tina also struck another problem: she couldn't mention anything about the threat made to her by a member of the outlaw motorcycle gang. This meant she was unable to explain why she had taken fourteen months to give her statement to police. Her credibility would be questioned.

The reason why the threat couldn't be mentioned was because of one of the earlier rulings made by Justice

Hulme and defence fears that the jury might believe Ross was affiliated with the bikie gang. Initially, the defence wanted to attack Tina over the time it took her to come forward.

During trials there are occasions when prosecution and defence counsels talk over the evidence and come to compromises. It's all part of the trial process. The defence wanted to know why Tina had waited so long, and when Wayne Creasey explained the situation to Carolyn Davenport, it became a huge problem. If the defence challenged Tina it would be known that Ross purchased drugs from a member of an outlaw motorcycle gang. This would then give the jury knowledge of Ross's drug addiction, which Justice Hulme had ruled as being prejudicial. Even if the drug connection was somehow kept out, the jury might have still drawn the inference that Ross belonged to or was affiliated with the gang in some way. Again, it could have been proven to be prejudicial.

During Tina's cross-examination Carolyn Davenport didn't ask why she had taken so long to give her statement, but very cleverly asked when was it she spoke to police about what she had heard and seen. Tina truthfully answered August 2001. It wouldn't have taken long for everyone in the courtroom to realise Tina had waited fourteen months before giving evidence. Tina was also questioned about her earlier statement, the one she gave police on the day of the murder, in which she stated that she had never heard Ross and Judith arguing.

Peter felt for Tina. It seemed so unfair. He was convinced of her sincerity and knew the jury and the judge would have understood if had she been able to explain why she was scared to say what she heard and saw that day. It wasn't to be, and Tina was left feeling distraught and thinking no one had believed her. As best as Peter tried to console her, the damage had been done. Tina's credibility had fallen victim to courtroom politics. Peter's only hope was that the jury had picked up the things he had during her testimony, that was, if Tina had made up her account of the Friday morning, 'she had a bloody good guess at the time of the murder'.

The moment came for Peter to take the stand. On 6 November 2003, Wayne Creasey invited Peter to explain what he saw on the afternoon of the murder. Peter described the commotion and Ross's bizarre behaviour as he swore at police and had earlier punched walls in a neighbour's house. The first record of interview Ross had given on that Friday night was played to the court in its entirety.

While the Clonmeen Circuit house appeared to have been broken into, the jury heard how, on closer examination, the discarded clothing and personal papers found in the main bedroom seemed to have been staged. Nothing had been stolen from the house, though Judith's handbag, purse, and keys, along with the swagman statue, were missing. Despite several searches and public appeals the missing items were never recovered. Police initially looked into the possibility that an intruder had broken into the house and was responsible for the murder, but there was no evidence to support such a theory.

Courtesy of the walk-through video taken four days after Judith's death, the jury saw Ross re-enact his movements on the day of the murder for Peter Fox and Graham Parker. Jury members were able to see for themselves Ross's lack of emotion and clinical behaviour when standing in the exact location where Judith's body had lain.

The third and final interview Ross gave police was also played. Regardless of the evidence presented to show Ross hadn't bought two bottles of beer on the Friday afternoon, he was sure he had and refused to admit that he hadn't. Throughout the interview, he kept coming back to the beer bottles, saying he was adamant he had purchased them from the pub. 'Well, Christ, you've shocked me ... I'll tell you now, I don't know what to say now, mate ... I honestly don't ... I was dead sure I bought them at the, the pub bottle shop ... I was, I was absolutely sure I bought them there'.

Ross couldn't account for why he drank excessively that day, or why he had changed his routine of picking up his eldest son from school. He claimed he didn't have to take his other son to league practice when arrangements had been made for him to do so, and he couldn't explain why he didn't call triple zero or run immediately for help after seeing his wife, but had the time to let his dog out the back door. 'I don't even know if I've gone into shock after I found my wife, because I've never been in shock before, I don't know, mate. I honestly don't, um, I do believe that I was in shock throughout this, I don't, don't know actually what shock is because I've never been in that situation before.'

The defence then had their opportunity. Peter knew he wouldn't have an easy time of it; he was, after all, the lead investigator, the one person responsible for putting the case together against Ross Brown. It had been Peter's decision to charge Ross and bring him to trial. It wasn't just the evidence being put under scrutiny; it was Peter's character. The defence would test nearly every aspect of Peter's case and he knew that the jury would be judging him, as a professional and as a person.

In anticipation of being asked if Ross was the only suspect, Peter had listed all the other suspects that were interviewed and, for one reason and another, ruled out of the investigation. He wasn't going to let the defence make out that Ross was the only person of interest.

Peter was fully prepared for his cross-examination. He was ready to rattle off names, dates and details of all the suspects; however, Carolyn Davenport didn't ask him about other suspects. She simply suggested that Peter had made up his mind that Ross was a suspect from the start, and that he had also decided then that Ross had committed the murder. Peter responded with, 'Yes and no … Yes he was a suspect, but no, I never made my mind up.'

Peter explained that, based on reports he had received when making his way to the crime scene that Ross was running around the street covered in blood and acting violently, he did believe Ross to be a suspect.

'Any detective worth his salt would have.'

But Peter never thought Ross had committed the murder until the investigation, in time, revealed evidence and eliminated other suspects, showing Ross to be the person responsible. It appeared the defence accepted there would have been a number of suspects.

Carolyn Davenport accused Peter of being 'obsessive' in his pursuit of her client. She put it to Peter that, 'You were prepared to do anything you could to find evidence to prosecute Ross Brown.'

Peter strongly denied he was anything but professional in his handling of the evidence, though the accusation that he had been obsessive did make him think. But he dismissed the idea, because throughout the investigation he never lost his objectivity. That was the difference between being passionate about a case and being obsessive in wanting to lock away someone. He always gave Ross the benefit of the doubt right up until the time the evidence eventually pointed to only one person being responsible for the murder of Judith Brown.

To test Peter's character, the defence played two to three minutes of the record of interview taken when Peter interviewed Joel on 27 November 2000. Justice Hulme had earlier ruled that neither Ross's boys nor his stepmother could give evidence or have their interviews shown without the consent of the defence. The defence elected to play only the few minutes they had selected. The whole interview ran for over an hour.

The selected segment showed Joel teary-eyed while being questioned by Peter. After playing it to the jury,

Carolyn Davenport asked, 'Well, detective, you're a pretty tough man. How did it feel bullying that young boy around?'

'It doesn't make me feel good to make that young boy upset at all,' Peter replied. 'I have a daughter, roughly the same age, and it's not lost on me. It was probably one of the toughest interviews I've ever had to do.'

Just as Peter was passionate about bringing Ross to justice, Carolyn Davenport and her team were equally passionate about proving their client's innocence. Peter didn't hold any malice towards Carolyn Davenport. She was doing her job to best represent her client.

～

One of the main pieces of evidence against Ross Brown was the fact there was nothing to support his claim that he had purchased the two long-necked bottles of Toohey's New on the Friday afternoon. To try to explain why police hadn't found any record of the purchase, the defence produced a photo taken by Crime Scene examiners of Ross's beer fridge in the garage of the Clonmeen Circuit home. On top of the fridge was a packet of cigarettes, which the defence believed to be a packet of Winfield, a popular brand of cigarettes. According to Carolyn Davenport, Ross had bought the two bottles of beer and a packet of Winfield blue. This was the reason why there was no record, because police had not looked any further than a receipt for two bottles when they needed to look for two bottles and a packet of cigarettes.

To the best of Peter's knowledge, Ross smoked roll-your-own cigarettes; Judith smoked tailor-mades, but not Winfield. To satisfy the court, Peter was excused to re-examine the sales receipts to see if there was a record of two bottles and a packet of cigarettes being sold at around the time Ross claimed he had made his purchase.

Peter spent days and evenings checking and rechecking the sales receipts from the two bottle shops in Anna Bay. He also contacted the company that makes Winfield to determine if the packet on top of Ross's beer fridge was indeed Winfield blue. Peter eventually spoke to one of the designers who gave evidence that the packet wasn't Winfield blue. The designer admitted there had been changes made to the packaging over the years, but he believed the photo didn't show a pack of Winfield. It was another brand of cigarette.

In addition, Peter could not find any record of purchase of two long-necked bottles of Toohey's New and a packet of cigarettes, irrespective of brand, during the afternoon of Friday 2 June 2000.

A week or so after Carolyn Davenport requested that hair samples taken from Judith's palms during the autopsy should be compared to Ross's and those belonging to Judith, a New South Wales Forensic Services Group scientific officer, Susan Bennett, appeared in court with the findings. After careful analysis Susan Bennett could not rule out the possibility that the strands of hair found on Judith's palms were those of Judith's husband, Ross Brown.

The scientific officer explained that, while the samples were different to those taken from Judith and Ross Brown, she could not exclude Ross as the source of the hair discovered during the autopsy. Nor could she exclude the hair as belonging to Judith. There was 'no significant difference' between the sample and Judith's own hair.

With regard to Ross's hair, Susan Bennett found the sample was lighter in colour than the strands taken from Ross for comparison. This meant little, however, as the hair colour could have changed over the past three years.

In short, the hair comparison was as Peter Muscio had thought it would be—inconclusive. It didn't help either the defence or the prosecution.

⌒

The Crown case against Ross Brown concluded on 20 November 2003. Justice Hulme invited the defence to present any witnesses or to re-examine any of the witnesses for the prosecution. They declined. Ross Brown's legal team elected not to call their client to give any testimony in his own defence.

Justice Hulme allowed Wayne Creasey and Carolyn Davenport to make their final addresses to the jury. Once the defence and prosecution rested, the trial judge explained to the jury their rights and obligations in coming to a verdict. He went over the various testimonies to summarise in an impartial manner all that had been presented over the past six weeks. His only criticism with any of the witnesses was the evidence given by Tina. While he wasn't suggesting that what Tina had to say was untrue, he didn't place a great weight on the evidence she gave.

Again, sitting in the back of the court, Tina began to cry. She felt the burden she had placed on the prosecution case by not being allowed to explain the threats. The whole experience, from the Friday of the murder through to her appearance in court, had done nothing but cause her great stress and sleepless nights. Still, Tina had put aside her own feelings and showed great courage in turning up to the court in support of Peter, the prosecution, and Judith's family and friends. Tina wanted to see justice done.

The jury retired on the afternoon of 25 November 2003. They would spend the remainder of that day and the whole of the next before returning to the court on 27 November with a verdict. It took the jury nine hours to run through all the evidence before a unanimous decision was reached.

Chapter 13

MOMENT OF TRUTH

With the jury retired to consider a verdict, Peter Fox felt quietly confident. The jury hadn't heard all the evidence Peter and his team had collected against Ross Brown, but Peter believed they had heard enough to prove Ross's guilt. Even after Justice Hulme's rulings before the trial and the defence doing its best to cast doubt over the remaining evidence, Peter thought Wayne Creasey had presented a strong and compelling case against Ross.

As stated, no one saw Ross commit murder and he had not made any admissions and a circumstantial case is not easy. For a circumstantial case to succeed the evidence must be strong, and this strength relies heavily on the thoroughness and professionalism of the officers collecting statements and physical evidence.

Although Peter was the one who eventually brought the case to trial, he couldn't have done it without the support of all the detectives and uniformed police who were part of Strike Force Saltpond. As much as Peter had been under scrutiny during the trial, so too was all the work that had been conducted by the numerous police officers in the first weeks of the investigation.

When word was received that the jury was ready to

give its verdict, Peter was filled with anxiety. His stomach churned. Peter had spent three years putting together all the evidence, he had spoken with family members, friends, and witnesses nearly every day during those years. Yet it wasn't always about the evidence. Peter would just be there for them, giving them a sympathetic ear and someone to share their grief with.

To say that Peter was passionate would be an understatement. He made no apologies for being so. He had given more than just his work time to solving Judith Brown's murder. That day, 27 November 2003, was a very emotional day for the detective sergeant, as it was for Judith's family and friends, and those witnesses who had stepped forward and assisted the investigation.

Hearing that the jury was ready, Peter made a call to Peter Muscio, who had been relocated from Maitland Police Station to Newcastle Police Station, where all the Crime Scene examiners are now based. Peter Fox was in a hurry to get out the door; he kept his message short. 'We've got a verdict. Get yourself down there!'

Newcastle Police Station is very near the Supreme Court, so Peter Muscio casually strolled from his office, even though his anticipation was as great as Peter Fox's. It had been an intense time, collecting and testing all the physical evidence, and having been grilled while giving his testimony. Peter shared his colleague's passion to see justice done.

Before entering the Newcastle Supreme Court, Peter Fox spoke to some of the family and friends. He asked them to remain calm and not let their feelings run away with them when the verdict was announced. Australian courts are very different from those normally seen in American dramas. Whichever way the verdict went, Peter didn't want anyone shouting or jumping about: Justice Hulme had the right to have those people removed from his court. Peter didn't want the day marred by news that anyone had been evicted from the Supreme Court.

Peter Fox and Peter Muscio sat at the back of the courtroom with Judith's relatives, friends, and the witnesses who had come to hear the verdict. On the other side of the court were Ross's two eldest boys and his stepmother.

Justice Hulme asked the jury foreman to deliver the verdict. The foreman stood and read one word, 'Guilty'.

It was over.

The elation Peter Fox thought he would have experienced when he arrested Ross was now surging. Tears welled in the eyes of Judith's family members and everyone hugged, shook hands, and gave kisses, while trying to remain as composed as possible so as not to disturb the judge. But it would have been impossible not to hear the joy and relief being expressed at the back of the courtroom.

Ross remained stone-faced. It wasn't until Justice Hulme began talking about the sentence hearing that Ross leaned forward, rested his head in his hands, and started to cry. Riley, Joel, and Gene had lost their mother, and now they had lost their father. The two older boys had attended court and, with their step-grandmother and a family friend, were ushered out the back way, away from the cameras and inquisitive journalists.

Walking out of the court, Judith's mother, Elfrieda put her arms around Peter and said in her thick German accent, 'Thank you. I can smile again.'

It was a moment Peter will never forget. Even years later, whenever Peter recalled Elfrieda's words, his emotion was obvious.

Speaking to journalists outside the court, Judith's family expressed their relief at finally having closure. The past three years had been mentally and physically draining on all concerned. They publicly thanked Detective Sergeant Peter Fox for his 'dedication and effort' in bringing Ross Brown to trial.

⁓

The sentence hearing was held on 6 February 2004. A victim's impact statement was presented by Judith's family, while Ross's defence made an application for special circumstances, asking Justice Hulme to consider leniency before passing sentence.

Justice Hulme heard of the devastating effect Judith's murder had had on her family, and how Elfrieda lit a candle every year on 2 June to remember her daughter and pray that justice would eventually be served on her killer.

Carolyn Davenport, still representing Ross Brown, told the court that the murder was a 'spontaneous act of aggression that was out of character'. She argued that her client deserved leniency because he did not have a history of violence, and because the murder had not been premeditated. While this may appear that Ross's legal team were admitting his guilt, the fact is that the defence must address a sentencing hearing having accepted the jury's verdict. However much the defence may disagree with it, a sentencing hearing is not the place to protest a client's innocence. Davenport also asked the judge to consider Ross's three boys, the closeness they shared with their father, and the milestones he would miss as they grew older. Carolyn Davenport argued that if Ross, who was nearly forty-seven at the time, were given a lengthy sentence he would be over sixty on release and find it almost impossible to secure work or a house.

Justice Hulme rejected the defence application.

In determining what sentence to impose on Ross, Justice Hulme accepted the jury's verdict but found the evidence did not suggest, beyond a reasonable doubt, that Ross had killed Judith with any premeditation or because of an argument, but there was still the probability. He also didn't believe, beyond a reasonable doubt, that Ross had intended to kill his wife, though the nature and number of injuries Judith received 'points in that direction'.

Justice Hulme did decide the murder did not fall into the worst category, meaning Ross would not be given life imprisonment. That sentence was reserved for those who kill solely for financial gain, with great cruelty, or multiple times. In conclusion he found, 'that no lesser non-parole period than I intend to impose provides an adequate reflection of the criminality involved in the prisoner's offence'.

Ross Ernest Brown was ordered to serve a maximum term of imprisonment of eighteen years, with a non-parole period of thirteen years and six months. This will entitle Ross to an early release on 10 January 2017, at which time he will be aged fifty-nine.

As at the verdict, journalists waited to speak with Judith's family after the sentencing hearing. Elfrieda, when she heard Justice Hulme pass sentence on Ross, broke down. She was satisfied with the outcome, but commented to the media, 'Judith would have lived longer than the eighteen years he got, but at least a judgment has been made'.

Ross is currently serving his sentence in the maximum-security wing of Lithgow Correctional Centre. It's a long way from Newcastle and Tanilba Bay. He still pleads his innocence and his boys support their father.

In a rare interview given to the *Newcastle Herald* in 2004, Riley, now a professional A-grade rugby league player, told the paper he believed his father was innocent of the murder. He has never discussed details with friends or his Newcastle Knights team mates. Everyone was aware of the basics.

After the trial the three boys were placed into the care of their step-grandmother, Ross's mother, at her home in Tanilba Bay. Because of distance, Ross writes letters and occasionally calls his boys. He also watches television whenever Riley is playing. Ross is very proud of his eldest son. Riley and his brothers remain very close and Riley in particular looks out for his two younger brothers.

In memory of his mother, Riley had a tattoo of a cross drawn on his arm. In the *Herald* interview he credits football and boxing as some of the things that have helped him deal with his anger over his mother's death and to get through the tough times. His brothers appear to be following in his footsteps, both being acclaimed as future stars of rugby league.

James Hooper from *The Sunday Telegraph* spoke with Riley, who had moved to Sydney to play for Eastern Suburbs, in March 2008. Again Riley maintained his father's innocence and described how he became his brothers' legal guardian at the age of eighteen, living on $200 a week while he saved his money to buy a house. He added that Judith's side of the family 'just brushed us completely, so that's pretty hard to deal with'. Riley also revealed an inscription he penned himself tattooed on his left shoulder that reads, 'A mother's love is always felt and a father's advice is never forgotten'.

～

Peter Fox has no doubt he caught the right man. Everyone involved in the case agrees. Such was the investigation that pieces of evidence would crop up throughout its duration, and as every piece was put together Ross Brown's guilt became more obvious.

Even four years after Ross's conviction, as Peter was going through the files, he came across another piece of evidence to add. It was an obvious one that had slipped past the attention of all the investigating police.

On the afternoon of the murder, a visible bloodstain was found on the tray of Ross's Toyota. It belonged to Floyd the dog. No one thought anything of it as Floyd had been allowed to run through the house, so it was assumed that he'd picked up blood on his paws as a result. Ross, on instruction from police, later secured the dog to the tray. It was thought that this was when the print had been left.

Looking at crime scene photos, Peter realised that Peter Muscio had to spray the entire carpet area and garage to highlight Floyd's bloodied prints because they could not be seen with the naked eye. How was it, then, that a very clear bloodied print was found on the tray? Peter now believes that this print was left in the morning, after Judith had been killed. Just another piece of circumstantial evidence.

～

In putting this book together Judith's family were contacted to be interviewed. They considered the invitation for a time but later declined it. At the time of writing, Ross Brown had been sent a letter care of Lithgow Correctional Centre asking for his input, but as yet no word has been received.

POSTSCRIPT

In the years Peter Muscio had served with the New South Wales Police Force as a Crime Scene examiner, he counts Judith Brown's murder as being the one that most affected him.

Peter remembers being taken with how clean and tidy the house was. In his experience most homes where murders occur appear unkempt, with dirty dishes filling the sink and rubbish lying around. There wasn't a speck of dust to be found in the Clonmeen Circuit home. On the night of the murder, Peter couldn't help but think that Judith was just a doting mother of three boys, whose sporting trophies and family photos adorned the different rooms. He imagined Judith yelling support and encouragement to her boys from the sideline, no matter how inclement the weather.

Judith cared for people. She had worked looking after the elderly and the young. The number of people who attended her funeral gave testimony to how easily she made friends.

Judith and Ross were an average couple, no different to people we all associate with. There was nothing in their lives that would have signalled such a dramatic turn of events. It was this, more than anything that made the murder so shocking.

Ross did not have a history of excessive violence and Judith would not have been considered a victim. While they obviously had their differences, and argued no more than most couples, for Ross to strike out and kill Judith was the worst of crimes.

In Peter Muscio's view for a father to kill the mother of his children is the lowest act. Ross had taken away the most precious thing in the lives of his boys and Judith can never be replaced.

By killing Judith, Ross had also devastated and divided a family. The boys sided with their father and were angry with their mother's family, who believed Ross was guilty. It was an outcome of the investigation that Peter Fox felt deeply about. He wished it had been different. But as he said, 'I can't fix that, that's not my job. I care about it, but I can't affect that. All I can do is what's right as far as the criminal law is concerned. That's my job as a professional.

'I will always believe it was the right decision. I have no doubt Ross Brown killed his wife.'

Judith's family accepted the verdict; they had their suspicions and were proved right. Ross's three boys continue to support their father and deny his guilt. Ross's action meant Elfrieda and her family not only lost Judith, but they also lost Judith's three boys.

Although the families are divided, what they share is the loss of a mother, a daughter, and a sister.